EFFECTIVENESS OF COMPUTER MODULES IN VALUE EDUCATION

(Educational Research)

Author

Dr. Sanjay Koriya
Harikrushna Nagar -2,
Jasdan, Dist. Rajkot, Gujarat

EFFECTIVENESS OF COMPUTER MODULES IN VALUE
EDUCATION
Author: Dr. Sanjay Koriya

■

■

ISBN: 978-93-5351-689-5

Price: Rs. 300=00

April, 2019 (First Edition)

Publisher : Dr. Sanjay Koriya

Printer : Shyam Computer, Junagadh

■

ACKNOWLEDGEMENTS

Research is a vital input in the process of development and changes whatever is the sphere of productive activity. The research required help and co-operation of many individuals. It is a matter of great satisfaction that the researcher could finish the work in due time with his keen sense of duty, sincerity and urgency. But, at this juncture, it is his pious duty to express his lings of gratitude to those who have helped him, co-operated him and motivated him. The researcher firmly believes that the credit goes to them for this research work.

I am fortunate enough to have an opportunity to work under the able guidance of Dr. A. K. Vyas. Without his help, this work could not have been possible. I, therefore, owe an enormous debt to him, not for his timely valuable guidance and parental care but for his deep insight and critical out-look with positive attitude.

Let me take this opportunity to extend my thanks to the Rai University, Ahmedabad that has given an opportunity to conduct this research work.

I am also thankful to all the experts for their valuable service, students their co-operation in the experiment.

I would like to thank all those who withstand by me and support me in the entire situation in completing the study.

Dr. Sanjay Koriya

Harikrushna Nagar -2,

Jasdan, Dist. Rajkot,

Gujarat.

Email: drkoriya@gmail.com

Cell: 9898001982

Dt. 08.03.19

Table of Contents

CHAPTER – 1
INTRODUCTION OF THE STUDY

1.1 INTRODUCTION

Values are most important treasure of our country which has strong cultural, ethical, moral, and spiritual foundations. This asset of values is passed from generations to generations and is embodied in the heart and soul of lacks of people of our country. Values are regarded desirable, important and held in high esteem by a particular society in which a person lives. Values reflect one's personal attitudes and judgements, decisions and choices, behaviour and relationships, dreams and vision. They influence our thoughts, feelings, and actions. They guide us to do the right things. Values are the guiding principles of life which are conducive to all round development. They give directions and firmness to life and bring joy, satisfaction and peace to life. Values are like the rails that keep a train on the track and help it to move smoothly, quickly and with direction. Values bring quality to life.

We can see growth, progress and development in all spheres of the society. Seemingly from outside everything seems to be fine and going on well. But if we do sonography of the society we will come to know that there is a severe problem which is needed to be rectified on war footing step. Misconception notion of modernity and rapid growth of science and technology and subsequent industrialization have caused a great threat and danger to our peace and values. In changed social set-up our definitions of good morals stand questioned. Human values and peace seem to be lost.

Now a day's newspapers, magazines and other news media are flooded with report of crime, murder, agitation, and eve-teasing. Incidents of violence and destruction are increasingly reported.

There seems one silver lining amongst the dark clouds of above said scenario and that is Education. Education is supposed to be a powerful instrument of change and progressive improvement of human behaviour. But now a day Education System is producing only Information Man. People are educated today but not civilized. In actual practice our Education System is doing very little to cultivate moral and human values in our youths and to promote national consciousness in the country.

The gulf between the content and aims of education is becoming wider day by day. The quality of teaching and teachers in our schools has now become a subject of the deepest national concern. It is the schools and homes where the primary attitudes and values towards social relationships and personal conduct get fixed and carried all through life. Unless the values we cherish are clearly defined and strongly and assiduously developed by all the agencies of Education, any educational system, no matter how elaborate or expensive, will fail in its aims. Education that does not help to promote Human Values and Virtues will not do any good to the society; it will rather mislead the entirety of humanity.

"The real difficulty is that people have no idea of what education truly is. We assess the value of education in the same manner as we assess the value of land or of share in the stock-exchange market. We want to provide only such education as would enable the student to earn more. We hardly give any thought to the improvement of the character of the educated. As long as such ideas persist there is no hope of our ever knowing the true value of education" – **Gandhi**

All cherished aims of any nation have been realized through the classrooms only. Butler Act of 1944 in U.K had a nice line written on top: *"What Our Schools Are, The Race Shall Be."* It is but natural to have great expectations from our classrooms. Our teachers and students very often fall short of our expectations because their personalities are developed mostly intellectually by assimilating and vomiting of the information (knowledge) and not by acquisition of moral and universal values. **International Commission on Education** has rightly pointed out that our education basically suffers from *"the gap between its content and the living experience of its pupils, between the system of values that preaches and the goals set up by society, between its ancient curricula and modernity of science"*.

The future destiny of a country rests not in the hands of soldiers and merchants but those of students and scholars. **Dr**

Annie Besant beautifully remarks, *"The destiny of a nation is folded within its budding youth as is the flower within the close embrace of the petal"*. Therefore a vigorous program for value education is the need of the hour.

Education opens up our mind, but value education gives us purity of heart too; education provides us with skills, but value education provides us sincerity too; education extends our relationship with the world, but value education links us with our own family members too. Education makes our livings better, but value education makes our life better too; education teaches us to compete with others, but value education encourage us to be complete too; education makes us a good professional, but value education makes us a whole human too; education takes us to the top, but value education takes the whole society on the top. Education gives us the capacity of better learning, but value education gives us the tool a deeper understanding too; education gives us *Anna* (food) but value education provides us *Ananda* too; education may bring limitations but value education is for liberation. After all, right education means *"Sa Vidya Ya Vimuktaye"*. It means that knowledge is what helps us to attain liberation.

The elements of value education can be found not only in the subject matter, but in the learning styles which are employed, the scheduling of the classroom, extracurricular activities, and parental involvement. Subjects like languages and social science are very rich sources of values. In fact the curriculum and syllabus of these subjects is designed keeping in mind the inculcation of values. While teaching these subjects in classrooms instructor has to cover the values also.

Mudaliar Commission, Secondary Education Commission (1952-53), Praksah Committee (1959), Kothari Commission (1964-66), National Education Policy (1986), National Curriculum for Elementary and Secondary Education (1988), Rammurti Committee (1990), all have stress on value oriented education.

The value education is therefore must be organized so as to secure the fullest possible development of body, mind, and heart; and a fruitful channelization of the life-energy in pursuits that contribute to the growth of both internal and external personality.

We are living in the era of technology where computers have become integral part & means to deliver education. Researches have proved that computer based teaching learning process yields much better results. Therefore researcher has prepared computer based modules for teaching values in supplementary Reader Book 'Lapwing' of English subject of standard XII and tested its effectiveness.

1.2 TITLE

In the present study researcher had titled the problem as:

Effectiveness of Computer Based Modules for Teaching of Values in the Supplementary Reader Book 'Lapwing' Subject of English of Standard – XII.

In the present study, the researcher had selected the Supplementary Reader book 'Lapwing' Subject of English, which was published by Gujarat State School Textbook Association, Gandhinagar. Researcher had identified & classified the values emerging from the above supplementary book. Researcher also prepared Computer Based Modules for teaching of values and tested its effectiveness.

1.3 OBJECTIVES OF THE STUDY

In any research objectives gives specific direction to study. In present study researcher had formulated objectives as:

1. To identify the reference sentences from the Supplementary Reader book 'Lapwing' of English subject of Standard XII.

2. To identify the values emerging from the Supplementary Reader book 'Lapwing' of English subject of Standard XII.

3. To identify the type of value, emerging from the Supplementary Reader book 'Lapwing' of English subject of Standard XII.

4. To classify values emerging, from the Supplementary Reader book 'Lapwing' of English subject of Standard XII.

5. To explain meaning of each value emerging from the Supplementary Reader book 'Lapwing' of English subject of Standard XII.

6.   To explain learning outcome of each value emerging from reference sentences from the Supplementary Reader book 'Lapwing' of English subject of Standard XII.

7.   To test the effectiveness of computer based modules for teaching of values emerging from Supplementary Reader book 'Lapwing' of English subject of Standard XII.

1.4 AREA OF THE STUDY

There are many areas of research. In the present study researcher identified and classified the values from supplementary Reader Book of English of Standard – XII, therefore it touches area of Value Education in Educational Philosophy. Also researcher had prepared computer based modules for teaching of values and tested its effectiveness, so it touches area of Educational Technology also.

1.5 TYPE OF THE STUDY

Based on the objective of the research, there are three types of study, which are as describing:

1. Basic Research
2. Applied Research
3. Action Research

In present study researcher prepared computer based modules for teaching and tested its effectiveness, therefore it is of applied research type.

There are two types of research which describe how the research is done. They are following:

1. Quantitative Research
2. Qualitative Research

In present study researcher had derived and classified values from the supplementary reader book of English subject of standard XII, and also prepared computer based modules for teaching of values and tested its effectiveness. Therefore it is of both type i.e. first part is qualitative and second part is quantitative.

1.6 HYPOTHESIS OF THE STUDY

Hypothesis of present study was,

There will be no significant difference between average value score obtained by students of Std. XII of pre-test and post-test as Value Clarification Test.

1.7 QUESTIONS OF THE STUDY

1. Which values are emerged from supplementary reader book 'Lapwing' of English subject of Standard XII?

2. How will the classification of the values done?

3. What will be meaning of emerged values?

4. What will be learning outcome of each value?

5.   How will be prepared computer based modules for teaching of values emerging from Supplementary Reader book 'Lapwing' of English subject of Standard XII?

6.   How will be tested the effectiveness computer based modules for teaching of values emerging from Supplementary Reader book 'Lapwing' of English subject of Standard XII?

1.8 VARIABLES OF THE STUDY

In the present research the variables and their category are shown as under:

1. Independent Variable. Independent variable is a variable which is manipulated or controlled or changed. It is a variable which is applied by researcher to measure change in other variable as its (independent variable) is measured on the other variable.

In the present research computer based module was the independent variable.

2. Dependent Variable. Dependent variable is the outcome variable and are the variable for which we calculate statistic. The variable which changes on the account of independent variable is known as independent variable.

In the present research value score of Value Clarification Test was the dependent variable.

3. Control Variable. Control variables are the variables which can influence dependent variable apart from independent variable, but researcher made them ineffective during the course of experiment.

When the researchers begins his experiment the thing which he must take care that during the experiment the researcher acquires the measurement of effect of only that variable the effect of which he wishes to examine. The effect of influencing variable is made ineffective during the course of the experiment.

In the present study control variables were: school, standard, subject, content matter, medium of study, and learning environment.

4. Intervening Variables. Influence of many variables are imaginary i.e. we cannot see their effect directly and cannot measure them. Such variables are called intervening variables. They intervene between cause and effect. It is difficult to observe, as they are related with individual feelings such as boredom, fatigue, excitement etc.

In the present study intervening variables were newness of experiment, like and dislike for values and individual differences among the students.

1.9 OPERATIONAL DEFINITION OF TERMS

Every research study involves certain key or technical terms which have some special connotation in the context of study; hence it is desirable to define such key words. Such definitions are known as operational definition of terms. A constitutive definition elucidates a term and perhaps gives some more insight into the phenomenon described by the terms.

In the present research, following terms were used by the researcher:

1. Value. Value means emerging good quality or qualities, from reference sentences of each reads of supplementary reader book of English subject of standard XII.

**2. Supplementary Reader Book `Lapwing'.** Supplementary Reader book `Lapwing' of English subject of Standard XII means, Supplementary Reader book of English for Standard XII, published by Gujarat State School Textbook Association, Gandhinagar – 2010.

3. Computer Based Module. Computer based module means, short duration computer based programs for teaching of values emerging from a read of 'Lapwing' supplementary reader book of standard XII.

4. Value Score VS-1. Value Score VS-1 means the score obtained by students in pre-test of Value Clarification Test.

5. Value Score VS-2. Value Score VS-2 means the score obtained by students in post-test of Value Clarification Test.

6. Effectiveness. Effectiveness means the significant difference between average value score of pre-test and post-test of Value Clarification Test.

1.10 IMPORTANCE OF THE STUDY

Each study has its own importance. In today's world when values are vanishing from our society, it is very important to revive values. Education is the best means to impart and inculcate values from childhood. This research is an attempt to design computer based modules to increase the awareness and retention of values from childhood.

In the present age when the computer has attained the place of best instrument for teaching of content of text books, it become necessary to know its fruitfulness in teaching of values also. For this computer based modules were prepared and checked how computer based modules are effective in value teaching and inculcation.

Present research will be useful in the following ways.

1. Students will know importance of values in life.

2. This research will be useful to the teachers to impart values while teaching supplementary reader book 'Lapwing' of English subject of standard XII.

3. This research will be useful to the future researchers. They will get knowledge of qualitative and quantitative research.

The results of the research and recommendations may lead them to select new directions of the research.

1.11 SCOPE OF THE STUDY

This research took up to test the effectiveness of computer based modules in teaching of values for the supplementary reader book 'Lapwing' subject of English for standard XII.

Computer based modules prepared and experiment conducted on selected reads of supplementary reader book 'Lapwing' of English of standard XII.

1.12 DELIMITATIONS OF THE STUDY

In any research, it is not possible to cover all aspects of area of interest, variables, population and so on. Thus a research has always certain limitations. Delimitations are those conditions which are beyond the control of the researcher that may play restriction on conclusions. Delimitation is a narrow term which indicates the boundaries of the study.

Present research is limited to the following aspects.

1. Present research was limited to Gujarati Medium Granted Schools of Rajkot district.

2. In present research convenience sampling method was used.

3. In present research one group pre-test and post-test experimental design was used.

8. Four Reads selected for value teaching.

9. Computer based modules prepared for value teaching.

10. Appropriate experimental design selected.

11. Experiment work conducted.

12. The analysis conducted through t-test.

13. With the help of statistical analysis null hypothesis tested.

14. The obtained results interpreted.

15. Appropriate implications prepared.

CHAPTER – 2
REVIEW OF RELATED LITERATURE

2.1 INTRODUCTION

Before taking up any kind of study, the related literature is acquired and studied to understand the problem. By review of the related literature the problem becomes clear and it direct the researcher in proceedings in his subject.

The literature in any field forms the foundation upon which all future work is done.

-P. R. Borg

Mr. H. G. Desai while explaining the importance of related literature states that, "review of the literature becomes necessary for the proper development of the problem." To prepare the background required for clarification and proper solution of the problem selected by a researcher the review of literature is essential.

The background of the problem can only be clarified if complete inference of related literature for understanding of research plan for problem development occurs. Mr. Agarwal while showing this type of importance states that, "by re-examination of the related literature, the researcher acquires the required understanding of work done so far.

Moreover the information regarding the facts, used by the researcher is also obtained by this kind of study.

By the review of related literature the researcher will be able to make:

1. The things to be included in a problem become clear.

2. The necessity to solve the problem by research can be understood.

3. Appropriate hypothesis to the problem can be prepared.

4. The source of information becomes clear.

5. Proper guidance regarding proper instruments and tools for collecting information can be   obtained.

This research was taken up to test the Effectiveness of Computer Based Modules for Teaching of Values in the Subject of English of Standard – XII. For this first of all, researcher identified the values emerging from the supplementary reader book 'Lapwing' of English of standard – XII. After identification values were classified and meaning of each value identified was explained. Then researcher prepared computer based modules for teaching of values for selected reads using movie maker software. Before implementation of program a pre-test was taken and after experiment post-test was taken as a Value Clarification Test.

2.2 THEORETICAL BASES OF THE STUDY

In this study the researcher had studied about identification of values and prepared computer based modules for teaching of values. So, the researcher had studied about values and computer based teaching modules under the following headings.

2.2.1   Meaning of Value

The meaning of value has different aspects according to the different subjects. Prof. W.S Arben defined value's as three characteristic in his book fundamental of Ethics", which is described by Desai in his book "Nitishashtra".

1. Value means that, which satisfy human desire.

2. Value is a biological factor reflects in psychological phase.

3. Which derives to development for soul or self-realization is itself value.

According to the dictionary (1988), 'value means something useful, qualitative or can be evaluated, that is 'price',' 'quality' or 'importance of thing.' According to Dave (1983) the English word 'Axiology' is derived from the Greek word 'Axious', which means 'value' 'proper for selection.'

According to Frenkle (1977), "Value is a thought, concept which means thought or concept about something important in life. When man values about something, it identifies something proper for something to do proper to to get."

According to Joshi (1975) operational definition "The meaning is given to thing by man, in that 'thing' is not important, but given meaning is important."

According to Gupta (1986), "Values are those standards or code for moral behaviour conditioned by one's cultural tenets and guarded by conscience, according to which human being is supposed to conduct himself and shape his life-pattern by integrating his belief, ideas and attitudes to realize cherished ideals and aims of life."

2.2.2   Classification of Value

Many experts had tried to list out the values and to classify various values in proper class. Many experts describe the classification as following.

1. Traditional and Functional values.
2. Relative and Non-Relative values.
3. Idealistic and Behavioural values.
4. Long standing values and Short Standing values.
5. Instrumental and Goal-centred values.

According to Joshi's approach (1995) of classification of values had given as follow (1) Personal Values (2) Social Values (3) Cultural Values (4) Economical Values (5) National Values (6) Moral Values (7) Aesthetic Values.

A study (NCERT) had given twenty three values list in a classification as describing.

1. Aesthetic Values: Truth, Equality or Religions, Devotion.
2. Moral Values: Duty, honesty, Abstinence, Character, Justice, Good Manner.
3. Social Values: Endurance, Social Justice, Equality, Co-operation, Humanity.
4. Economical Values: Production.
5. Bodily Values: Health.
6. Biological Values: Self-protection, Food.

7. Political Values: Patriotism, Democracy.

8. Global Values: Brotherhood, Human Vision, Human Right.

N.L.Gupta had described classification of values in his book "Human Values in Education", which were as describing.

1. Economic Values. An object has economic value if it commands a money price. It is a common place that we do not value money or material thing for their own sake, but rather for the enjoyment they make possible. Economic value is instrumental rather than intrinsic, although the miser may get a genuine and perhaps unique satisfaction from the mere handling of his money.

2. Health, Bodily and Recreational Values. Under this heading we shall include the values of health or physical well-being, play and all the satisfactions that comes from the gratification of bodily needs, such as hunger, thirst, rest and sex.

3. Social Values. The satisfaction we get from friendship, love, family and membership in groups are to be included in the social values.

4. Moral Values. These are the satisfaction and dissatisfactions that accrue to the individual in the course of his attempts to make right choices.

5. Aesthetic Values. Perceived object to which the adjectives beautiful and ugly are relevant give rise in the observer the kind of experience we call aesthetic.

7.   Intellectual Values. We prize or get satisfaction from attaining truth in any of its forms. We say that an object or action has intellectual value if it in some way helps or hinders the findings of truth.

8.   Religious Values. If an object by virtue of its relation to the divine can be called holy or sacred, it is said to have a religious values, and the experience of such objects as sacred or divine is called a religious experience.

Each value area has a subjective and an objective aspect. Sometime we speak of the value as meaning the individual's experience of satisfaction and sometimes value refers to some property or quality of the object or of a fact. This is so because value is a relation between an organism and an object, although we cannot ever be sure just how much each contributions to the transaction.

In order to create new social order Gandhiji introduced Nai Taleem in the year 1937, which is popularly known as Basic Education.

The NCERT and Gandhi Peace Foundation had jointly sponsored and studied on Gandhian values at the school stage. These were the values which he practiced himself in his personal and public life, experimented with them and suggested that our society should be instructed on the basis of these values if we want to remodel the social setup through education. These values are as follow. (1) Truth (2) Non-violence (3) Freedom (4) Democracy (5)

Sarva dharma sambhav (6) Equality (7) self-realization (8) Purity of ends and means (9) self-discipline (10) Cleanliness.

2.3 COMPUTER TECHNOLOGY IN THE FIELD OF EDUCATION

The computer is being used at different levels in educational process. Before looking at the uses and advantages of computer based teaching let us acquire some primary clarification of computer technology.

2.3.1   Constitution of Computer

Computer is an electronic instrument which is used to make calculation and control such processes. The computer has three parts.

1. Input unit
2. Output unit
3. Central processing unit

To get the work done by the computer it is necessary to provide information. The device which provides information are known an input unit or input device which include keyboard, mouse, scanner, microphone etc.

Central processing unit (CPU) is the main part of computer in which the control unit takes decisions about the processing of incoming information and come out with results. In short, it controls the processes of computer.

During the controlling of the process the ALU Arithmetical Logical Unit and memory unit becomes helpful. The arithmetical logical unit performs arithmetical and logical processes whereas the storage of memory required for these messages is done by memory unit. In the memory unit HDD hard disk drive and FDD floppy disk drive are involved. Higher the hard disk of a computer, grater will be its capacity to store the matter.

There is an arrangement of units for storage of information which are set in the form of hard disc drive (HDD), floppy disk drive (FDD) and compact disk drive (CDD) which sequentially administer the hard disc. The hard disk has more storage capacity but its memory cannot be moved from one place to another. Memory in floppy can be moved easily but its storage capacity is less. The limitation of these two can be removed in compact disk, that is, the storage capacity of compact disk is more and can be carried easily. Therefore most of software are prepared on compact disk.

The instruments used to bring out results prepared by the computer is called output device. It includes monitor, speaker, printer etc.

2.3.2   Computer System

Computer is an electronic device. The coordination among different parts of a computer is essential. This coordination needs a system. This computer system has three parts (i) Hardware (ii) Software (iii) Live ware.

The computer hardware includes input device, output device and central processing unit. The software is used for hardware. The software does not have physical existence. It is a collection of instructions about the work to be done by a computer.

Different types of people such as computer programmer, computer manufacturer and computer user involved with computer are included in live ware.

2.3.3   Computer Software and its type

Instructions are given to the computer for variety of work it does. These instructions are clear, logical and in sequence. Computer software is a collection of instructions which are prepared with the arithmetical and logical capabilities of HDD of computer, to obediently follow the instructions accordingly. The hardware is of no importance without software. The software activates the hardware. There are three types of software, (i) operating software (ii) application software and (iii) utility software.

1. Operating System (OS)

It is also called operating system. It is a collection of machine based programmes which act as an interphase that is interpreter between application software computer and computer hardware. The main function of operating software is an all-round administration or management of the computer.

There are two types of operating system for personal computer (i) DOS (ii) Windows. DOS (disk operating system) is a single user single tasking operating system in which character / text based instruction or commands are used, whereas window is a window based operating system which is actually an extension of capabilities of DOS. Window is a graphical user interphase (GUI).

Multitasking provides the facility of multi-tasking and gives on line help.

2. Application Software

The user for the different works such as writing letters, arranging files, looking after financial dealings, drawing pictures, making calculations, doing statistical analysis and watching films uses softwares which are called application softwares. There are two types of application software (i) for general use and (ii) for specific purpose.

The software for general use are called by the name of packages which are being sold in readymade form for the use. It provides facility of menu based management. There is a facility of help of tools which are application software. These tools include MS word, MS excel and MS power point.

The software for specific purpose are made by programmer according to the task required. The software developed for such purpose is called tailor made software.

3. Utility Software

The work efficiency of a computer is on decline; especially the computer virus and disc fragmentation lowers the work efficiency of computer. The software used for making the computer efficient again is called utility software. Disc fragmentation software is used to repair the disc fragmentation from computer virus. These software are utility type software.

2.3.4 Uses of Computer in the field of Education

The use of computer in distance education and classroom teaching is increasing day by day. The computer is specifically used in education in the field of teaching learning, drilling and practicing, for adaptation, for learning through trial and error, for acquiring knowledge through games for evaluation of teaching learning process, for marking and analysis and for imparting value education.

1. Teaching – learning

In this approach, the content to be learnt is divided into small parts. To check out whether the student has understood the content or not, questions are asked to him at the end of each part. The answers are being interpreted by the computer and then appropriate feedback is provided. This role of computer is similar to programmed learning. The programmes in the form of linear programming and branch programs can also be prepared in computer.

2. Drill work and practice

The theories or law learnt by the students are provided with many reference examples. Whether the student has understood the theories or laws is examined. Feedback is provided to correct and after providing treatment to wrong response, subsequently the students are sent to the extent of effective learning by the computer.

3. Adaptation

In teaching subjects like science the graphical presentation of the topics like understanding of laws of speed, process of nuclear fission, and principles of gravitation becomes very difficult. By providing adaptation through computer and by showing example based on laws, the drill work of concept can be done.

4. Teaching through trial and error

In teaching some subjects students are allowed to work on their own. The mistakes or error done by the students is tolerated. They come to know the error and are asked to solve them. After some time they will be able to solve and then are allowed to proceed further. This is the method of teaching through trial and error.

5. Knowledge through computer assisted games

In this the role of a computer becomes that of a partners of the learner or evaluator of the learner. The vocabulary or general knowledge can be improved through this technique.

6. Evaluation in teaching learning process

By collecting the questions corresponding to the subject, keeping in mind a particular structure of the questions of equal difficult value, can be obtained through computer.

7. Marking and analysis

The responses of the student can be marked and not only that, on the basis of scoring, the sections of test can be analyzed, and by that the efficiency of the students can be analyzed.

8. Imparting value education

The values which are imbibed in content can be reinforce in the student by showing them small clips contains importance of that value. Also short moral stories, character sketch, and small movies can be shown on computer to increase value awareness in students.

2.4 THE ADVANTAGES OF COMPUTER BASED TEACHING

The advantages of computer based teaching are as describing.

1. The student can do self-learning with self-speed.
2. During the teaching learning through computer the learner gets continuous response, thus the teaching work become live.
3. Immediate feed-back suitable to given response can be obtained.
4. According to the programmed learning as given by Skinner, the content can be defined into small parts (module), and subsequently one can proceed further.
5. Students can easily carry the computer to his room, hostel, tutorial room etc.
6. Learning stages can be arranged according to the time schedule.
7. Student can learn on his own and in his own ways.

2.5 THE DISADVANTAGES OF COMPUTER BASED TEACHING

1. It is more expensive.

2. Every teacher cannot prepare computer based teaching program.

3. Due to shortage of professionals having sound knowledge of educational psychology and education technology, it becomes difficult to prepare such programs.

4. It takes long time to prepare computer based teaching programs.

5. Teachers who do not have sufficient knowledge about computer generally avoid using such programs.

6. Interaction between teacher and students lessens down in computer based teaching.

7. Students do not get any other knowledge apart from content of program.

Though limitations are there but if proper care is taken to avoid them than computer based learning becomes a boon and can make learning more interesting and increases retention power.

2.6 PRACTICAL BASES OF THE STUDY

Identification and selection of a research problem cannot be done without reviewing the related literature because it gives an idea to the researcher that what work had already been done on the subject of his choice and what remains to be done. Review of literature may guide the researcher to modify the existing knowledge on the subject. The main objectives of a review of the related literature are as describing.

1. The review of the literature is the basis of most of the research projects in the physical sciences, natural sciences, social sciences, education and humanities.

2. A review of the related literature gives the researcher an understanding of the previous work that has been done.

3. The results of the review actually provide the data used in research.

4. A review of the literature would develop the insight of the investigator. The information thus, gained will save the researcher's much of time.

5. A review of the related literature can help the researcher in making him alert to research possibilities that have been overlooked.

6. The review of the literature provides us with an opportunity of gaining insight into the methods, subject and approaches employed by other researchers. This will lead to significant improvement of our research design.

7. A careful consideration of the chapters entitled recommendations for further research, in various research studies guide us regarding the suitability of a problem and in assisting us delimiting our research problems.

The researcher went through past studies to make the research accurate and particular. The summaries of studies obtained from past researched are given here.

Chavda (1995) had worked for qualiy emerging from children stories of Gijubhai Badheka. The objectives of the study of M.Ed. level as describing: (1) To examine which qualities are emerging from every story created by Gijubhai Badheka. (2) To select the stories which have qualities more than one from stories created by Gijubhai Badheka.

The researcher included part-1 to 10 of stories created by Gijubhai Badheka as population. These parts accepted as a sample. The story analysis care was used for the study. Analysis was done by qualitative method.

Total 24 qualities were seen in reference to stories created by Gijubhai Badheka as finding. (1) Love (2) Brave (3) Unity (4) Clever (5) Service (6) Value (7) Work (8) Brotherhood (9) Honesty (10) Joy (11) Simplicity (12) Polite (13) Satisfaction (14) Honesty (15) Cleanliness (16) Imagination (17) Truth (18) Self Observation (19) Observation (20) Environment Recognition (21) Help (22) Loyalty (23) Modest (24) Patience

Dave (2005) had worked for comparison of educational achievement of 'Aamnondh' unit of standard XI Account subject. The objectives of the study were as Ph.D. level as describing. (1) To compare educational achievement of 'Aamnondh' unit of standard XI account subject by work card, computer aided teaching and lecture method.

Computer aided teaching and lecture methods of teaching were used. The students of **standard** XI were included in population. Total 45 students were included in sample. Computer aided program was made for study. Experimental method was used. F-test was used for analysis.

Findings of the study were as describing. (1) Computer aided program and work card method was equally effective in boys and girls. (2) Lecture method was more effective in boys and girls compare to computer aided program.

Gandhi (2009) had worked prepare computer based teaching material and test its effect on educationally backward students for teaching the units in the text books for Mathematics subject in primary school. The objectives of the study were as Ph.D. level as describing. (1) To prepare computer based teaching material in text books for the standard VIII. (2) To evaluate the effectiveness of computer based teaching material in reference to educationally backward students.

Formal and informal methods of teaching were used. The students of standard VIII were included in population. Computer based program was mad for study. Convenience Sampling Method was used. t-test was used for analysis.

Findings of the study were as describing. (1) Computer based program was effective in the Maths achievement.

Gohel (2002) had worked for Educational philosophies emerging from Upnishada. The objectives of the study were as Ph.D. level as describing. (1) To study the various values in Upnishada. (2) To make the Shlok Analysis Card for study of educational philosophies of the Upnishada.

Content analysis method and Qualitative Analysis method were used for analysis.

Findings of the study were as describing. (1) Teaching is objective oriented process. (2) In teaching learning process connection between pre knowledge and present content is very important. (3) Knowledge is reinforced by repetition. (4) Concentration is required in teaching learning process.

Joshi (2002) had worked for the value identification and the effectiveness of value identification model for teaching the units in the text books for Gujarati subject in secondary school. The objectives of the study were as Ph.D. level as describing. (1) To study the various values in text books for the standard VIII, IX and X. (2) To make the teaching program for selected five values humanity, nationality, courage, love for nature and consideration for other in reference to develop value identify and value justify by traditional method. (3) To make the teaching program for selected five values humanity, nationality, courage, love for nature and consideration for other in reference to develop value identify and value justify by value identification model. (4) To evaluate the effectiveness of value identification model and value justification in reference to selected five values.

Formal and informal methods of teaching were used. The students of standard VIII, IX and X were included in population. Total 511 students were included in sample. Value identification test was mad for study. Survey and experimental methods were used. t-test and covariance were used for analysis.

Findings of the study were as describing. (1) Fifteen values identify were found from the fifty six units of standard VIII textbook with expert's view. (2) Sixteen values identify were found from the fifty six unites of standard IX textbook with expert's view. (3) Seventeen values identify were from the sixty five units of standard VIII textbook with expert's view. (4) value identification model was proved effective than traditional method in some values development.

Khaniya (1999) had worked for values emerging from the stories of Panchatantra. The objectives for this study of M.Ed. level as describing. (1) To examine which values are emerging from the stories of Panchatantra created by Pandit Vishnu Sharma. (2) To know the values subtype from value emerging from the Panchatantra.

The translation of Sanskrit in Gujarati published of Pandit Vishnu Sharma's Panchatantra. From this book he took sixty three stories as a population for this study. For selection of sample, researcher selected forty stories out of sixty three stories of Panchatantra created by Pandit Vishnu Sharma. The investigator prepared a record card with different points. Qualitative research's Content Analysis method was used for the study. So by qualitative method the analysis was done.

Finding of the study was from forty stories of Panchatantra as describing: (1) Twenty values were identified which were divided into five types from forty stories of panchantantra.

Rose (2005) had worked for the effectiveness of computer assisted teaching software in low achievement of students in the text books for mathematics subject in IX standard. The objectives of the study were as Ph.D. level as describing. (1) To make the computer assisted teaching software (2) To evaluate the effectiveness of Computer assisted Teaching Software.

The students of standard IX was included in population. Experimental method was used. t-test and covariance were used for analysis.

Findings of the study were as describing. (1) Computer aided program was found effective in students of low achievement

2.7 REVIEW OF PAST RESEARCHES

The researcher had prepared the following questions for related review which were as describing.

1. Who was researcher?

2. Which level the study was taken?

3. In which university the work was done?

4. When this research work was done?

5. Who was selected for the study?

6. Which was the size of the sample?

7. Which was the method of the sampling?

8. Which tool was used?

9. Which research method was used?

10. Which method was used for data analysis?

11. What were the findings of the researches?

The answers of these questions were given in the table 2.1 named the table of the past researches from the following pages.

2.8 CONCLUSION OF THE REVIEW

The objective of this study was to identify the values emerging from supplementary reader book of English subject of standard XII and to prepare computer based modules for teaching of values. According to that, researcher reviewed past researches at various levels. The summaries of past researches are as describing.

- Total seven researches were studied, of which two were of M.Ed. level and five were of Ph.D. level.

- These researches were done at various subjects like Gujarati, Mathematics, and Accounts. Apart from the above subjects Children Story Book of Gijubhai Bhadheka, Stories of Panchtantra by Vishnu Sharma and Upnishada were also taken.

- Out of total seven researches three researches were qualitative and four researches were experimental.

- Out of total seven researches, content analysis method was used in three researches, t-test was used in three researches, F-test was used in one research.

- Tools like Value Identification Test, Computer Based Program, Story Analysis Card, Sholak Analysis Card, and Computer aided Program, Computer assisted Program were used in the above researches.

Results of past researches are as describing.

1   Computer Based Learning was more effective than traditional method.

2   Computer Based Learning was also more effective in low achiever students.

3   Computer Based Learning was more effective in Social Science, Chemistry, Mathematics and Gujarati.

2.9 SIGNIFICANCE OF THE RESEARCH

The significance of the present research was as describing.

1. Qualitative and quantitative both methods were used.

2. Content Analysis and experimental method were used.

3. The research was done on students of standard XII.

4. The research was conducted on the subject of English at Higher Secondary level.

5. One group Pre-Test and Post-Test design was used.

6. Modern software of computer – Movie Maker, Power Point was used in the research.

7. Computer Based modules were prepared for Teaching of Values.

CHAPTER – 3
RESEARCH DESIGN AND METHODOLOGY

3.1 ORIGIN OF THE STUDY

Values are the base of Indian culture and identification of Indian society. But since last few decades there are many sentences which are prevailing in society.

- We are educated but not civilized.
- Wildlife is decreasing in woods and increasing in cities.
- Our education system is producing only information men not cultured and civilized citizens.
- The tragedy of war is that it uses men's best to do men's worst.
- Today human has forgotten humanity.

Researcher gave a deep thought on the above sentences and many more such sentences and tried to find out the root cause of such problems. It was found that lack of value education is the root cause and if we do not take any measures in this regard then the situation will become worse. So it becomes necessary to work on this area at war footing steps.

Also today computer technology has become integrated part of education system. Through educational technology not only content can be imparted more but also it engages the concentration and interest of the students.

In the present times so many researches are done in different areas. Each area has its own importance. The chief aim of the education is to produce good global citizens, who live a life acceptable by the society. When a child starts schooling, he is given some syllabus for study particular subjects. Total schooling is based on the syllabus. Teacher teaches with a focus on syllabus and students learn anything from the point of view of syllabus or anything around the syllabus area. So, subject books are of utmost importance during schooling. Because of this importance, subject books are constructed with a motive of all-round development for which values becomes essential part of the syllabus.

During early childhood the values are inculcated through morals of stories and then as a child moves to primary and secondary it is the right time for value inculcation through all subjects. So, syllabus books must each different kind of values directly or indirectly. Subjects like Literature – English, Hindi, Gujarati and Social Science are good source of values. For this reason researcher choose the supplementary reader book 'Lapwing' of English subject of standard XII, derived the values from it and prepared computer based modules for teaching of values.

3.2 POPULATION OF THE STUDY

The one and only aim of any researcher is to find out the conclusions that can be applied universally. But the concept of population is very vast itself and it is quite impossible to make study on the whole population itself. Due to such reasons the researcher had limited the size of population for accuracy in work.

In present study students of standard XII of higher secondary level of Gujarati medium granted schools in academic year 2015–16, of Rajkot District selected as population.

Besides, 'Lapwing' Supplementary Reader book of standard XII for Gujarati medium was population of the study.

3.3 SAMPLE OF THE STUDY

A sample is a small proportion selected for observation and analysis. It is a group representing the population. The selection of the sample and the size of the sample are based on the design of the study, the size of the population and accuracy of experiment.

In this study, values identified from supplementary reader book Lapwing's first ten Reads and computer based modules prepared for First Four Reads.

For convenience in experiment, and co-operation from school management, Principals, Teachers and Students regarding the experiment, standard XII of three higher secondary Gujarati medium schools of Jasdan Taluka and Vinchhiya Taluka was chosen. By convenience sampling method these schools were chosen.

The schools are:

1. Shree Vivekanand Vinay Mandir, Jasdan: Where Pre-Piloting was done on 20 students.

2. Shree M.B. Ajmera High School, Vinchhiya: Where the main experiment was conducted on 35 students.

3. DSVK High School, Jasdan: Where the repetition of experiment was conducted on 35 students.

3.4 RESEARCH METHOD

Research method is an important part of study process. In the planning process, the researcher had decided about research method that could use in solving the research problem. There are three types of research methods.

1. Historical Research Method
2. Descriptive Research Method
3. Experimental Research Method

The historical method is used to derive general conclusion after solving the problem by scientific method for understanding present situation in context of past situation.

After knowing present situation on the basis of that, for future decisions and evaluating present situation with ideal situation any one of the descriptive methods is used to solve the problem by scientific method.

If one variable affects the other, then the experimental research method is applied to examine the purpose of that effect.

In present study researcher had identified and classified values from the supplementary reader book 'Lapwing' of English subject of standard XII, and had also prepared computer based modules for teaching of values and test its effectiveness. Therefore it was of both type i.e. first part is descriptive and second part is experimental.

3.4.1 Descriptive Research

A descriptive research has four methods.

1. Survey method

2. Content analysis method

3. Co-relation method

4. Development method.

From the above the researcher had selected content analysis method of descriptive research for this study.

Content analysis is one of the important methods of descriptive study. In order to arrive at result from the collected data, it is necessary to classify it. Content analysis is the reproduction of data into categories. It is a methodology for determining the content of written, recorded, or published communications via a systematic, objective and quantitative data. According to Kalpan,

"Content analysis attempts to characterize the meaning in a given body to discourse in a systematic and quantitative fashion"

In the present research, the following steps were selected for content analysis.

1. Clarification of objectives. In the present study, the objectives were to identify the different values and classification of those values from the supplementary reader book 'Lapwing' of English subject of standard XII.

2. To classify the values. In the present study, the classification of values was done according to the definition of the philosophers and past researches of value education.

3. Sampling of the book. First Ten Reads of the supplementary reader book Lapwing of standard XII were selected for the study.

4. Reading the Reads. The researcher had read first ten Reads in reference with values in this study.

5. Identification of reference sentences. Researcher had separated out those sentences from which values were emerging.

6. Identification of value. After identification of reference sentences researcher had identified value or values from it.

7. Identification of value type. After identification of value, researcher had found out its type, for this reference from the various books of value education and past researches were taken.

8. Classification of value. After finding value type researcher classified all values.

9. Explanation of meaning of value. Each value which was identified was given a meaning to understand it in a better way.

10. Finding learning outcome of each value. Learning outcome of each value was found. For this help of expert was taken.

For step five to step ten the researcher had taken the help of expert opinion by giving them record sheets. After compiling all the opinions researchers did the final classification of the values emerging from the supplementary reader book 'Lapwing' of English subject of standard XII.

3.4.2 Experiment Research

The experimental method in education is the application and adaptation of the classical method of experimentation. It is a scientifically sophisticated method. It provides a method of investigation to derive the basic relationship among phenomena under controlled condition or, more simply, to identify the conditions underlying the occurrence of a given phenomenon. Experimental research is the description and analysis of what will be, or what will occur, under carefully controlled conditions.

Experimenters manipulate certain stimuli, treatments, or environmental conditions and observe how the condition or behaviour of the subject is affected or changed. Such manipulations are deliberate and systematic. The researchers must be aware of the other factors that could influence the outcome and remove or control them in such a way that it will established a logical association between manipulated factors and observed factors.

Experiment research provides a method of hypothesis testing. Hypothesis is the heart of experimental research. After the experimenter defines a problem he has to propose a tentative answer to the problem or hypothesis. Further, he has to test the hypothesis and confirm or disconfirm it.

3.4.3 Characteristic of Experiment Research

The experimental research is an arranged situation, gives appropriate results regarding the effect of specific method. To find an appropriate solution to a problem through experimental research these types of characteristics are considered essentials.

1. Control on variables. During experiment on dependent variable, some variable influences automatically, so the fear of result of research being polluted arises. Therefore to maintain the reliability of the experiment, the researcher identifies such variables and controls them by different methods.

In the present research variables like school, standard, subject, content matter, medium of study, and school environment which effect on dependent variable were identified. It was tried by researcher to keep these variables in control.

2. The implementation of Independent Variable. The researcher identifies the variables which influence on dependent variable and after controlling those implements the dependent variables. He studies the relationship between independent variable and dependent variables. Appropriate method and program suitable to the purpose is organized.

In this research the independent variable was computer based teaching modules, for the implementation of which the experimental work was organized.

3. Measurement of Dependent Variable. In this research the researcher examines the effect of independent variable on dependent variable. After applying independent variable the researcher measured dependent variable with the help of appropriate instrument and examines the effect of independent variable.

The dependent variable in this research was value score of post-test as a Value Clarification Test.

4. Repetition of Experiment. By repetition of experiment through same method the validity expansion, generalization, and reliability of the result is enhanced.

The repetition is also included in the experimental research. For this an experiment is conducted on students of standard XII of DSVK High School, Jasdan.

3.5 EXPERIMENTAL DESIGNS

Experimental design is an important aspect of experiment. Time, method, revision and validity of work can be determined by the experimental design. This way design is a blueprint of whole experiment for experimenter. Which type of design is to be selected depends on the objectives of experiment. Experimental designs are of three types.

Pre Experimental Designs	Pure Experimental Designs	Partly Experimental Designs
1. One study group	1. Two groups incidental subjects' post-test design.	1.Unmatched controlled group pre-test and post-test design
2. One group pre-test – post-test design	2. Two groups incident paired subjects' only post-test design.	2. Counter balanced group design
3. Two group design	3. Two incidental group pre-test – post-test design.	3. Periodical design
	4. Solomen incidental four group design	
	5. Factorial Design	

3.5.1 Experimental Designs of Present Research

In the present research after identification and classification of values computer based modules for teaching of values were prepared and its effectiveness was tested. Keeping this objective in mind one group pre-test, post-test design was selected.

One group pre-test, post-test design

Group	Pre-test	Treatment	Post-test	Effectiveness
Experimental Group (E)	T_1	Computer based modules (X)	T_2	$H_0 : T_1 = T_2$

3.6 PLANNING IN CONTEXT OF EXPERIMENT

The effect of independent variable on dependent variable was to be measured in this research. Independent variable was computer based modules for teaching of values.

For this Four Reads from supplementary reader book of English of standard XII were selected. (1) The Birdman of India, (2) Her Words, His Vision, (3) Final Game, (4) I Love me. Students were taken to computer laboratory. Firstly they were given pre-test where they expressed their views about the values which were identified from that particular Read. Then with the help of projector the Read was taught by computer based program prepared in software of movie maker.

Along with the content all reference sentences were shown, which values were identified from that was shown, meaning of values were shown and finally a small clip about that value was shown to teach them that value. The students were able to see and listen what was spoken and shown. This way the students were listening and also observing the topics shown to them. When it was necessary the repetition was done. After the satisfaction of the students the new topic was taught. At the end of each Read, post-test was given where the students wrote their understanding about the shown values.

3.7 RESEARCH TOOLS

For each and every type of research we need certain instruments to gather new facts or to explore new fields. The instruments thus employed as means for collecting data are called tools. The selection of suitable tools is of vital importance for successful research. Different tools are suitable for collecting various kinds of information for various purposes. The researcher may use one or more of the tools in combination for his purposes. Therefore it becomes very much necessary that a research students should familiarized themselves with the varieties of tools.

In qualitative research tools like interview, dialogue, description, record sheets, opinionnair are used. In the present research the researcher had constructed opinionnair, record sheets and Value Clarification Test.

3.7.1 **Opinionnaire.** Eighty three values were given by NCERT was taken as base for value identification. These values and its type described in the opinionnair. It was made according to following steps.

Step – 1 Reading of reference literature. The literature of values and its classification were read in the first step. The books related to values and their types were read and their names were given in the references.

Step – 2 Construction of primary opinionnair. In the second step, the primary opinionnair was constructed.

Step – 3 Expert's view and final opinionnair. In this step, the opinions of experts were taken. Expert's request letter was given in appendix – I and expert's name were given in appendix – VI. After taking the expert opinion, final opinionnair was constructed and it was given in appendix - I.

3.7.2   Record Sheets. Record sheets were constructed in the study according to following steps.

Step – 1 Reading of reference literature.   The past researches of values were read in the first step.

Step – 2 Construction of primary record sheets. The primary record sheets had contained following points.

1. Read Number.
2. Read Name
3. Content of Read
4. Reference Sentences
5. Emerging Values
6. Value Type
7. Interpretation
8. Learning Outcome
9. Expert Remark

Step – 3 Expert views and final record sheets. In this step, the opinion of experts was taken. Expert request letter was given in appendix – II and experts names were given in appendix – VI. Experts had given suggestion and those changes had been done in final record sheets. After taking the opinion of the experts, the final record sheets were constructed.

3.7.3   Value Clarification Test

Before starting chapter researcher gave Value Clarification Test as a pre-test to the students and after applying of independent variable post-test was taken. The format of both tests was same. The construction of Value Clarification Test was done according to following steps.

Step – 1 Reading of reference literature. The literature related to construction of Value Clarification Test was read and also references from past researches were taken.

Step – 2 Construction of primary Value Clarification Test. In the second step, the primary Value Clarification Test was constructed.

Step – 3 Expert Opinion and final Value Clarification Test. In this step, the opinions of expert were taken. Expert's request letter was given in appendix – III and expert's name were given in appendix – VI. Experts had given suggestion and those changes were inculcated in Value Clarification Test and final Value Clarification Test was constructed and it was given in appendix – IV.

3.8 COLLECTION OF DATA

In the present research the objective of researcher was to derive values, classify them, preparation of computer based modules for teaching of values and to test its effectiveness through Value Clarification Test. Data was collected with the help of experts, teachers and students in the form of opinionnair, record sheet and Value clarification test.

3.9 FORM OF DATA

In the present research the data collected by the researcher was of both types i.e. qualitative and quantitative. Data from opinionnair and record sheet was in the form of qualitative data, while the data collected from Value Clarification Test was quantitative in nature.

3.10 ANALYSIS OF DATA

In the present research, researcher identified and classified values from the supplementary reader book of English of standard XII with the help of opinionnair and record sheet. Content analysis method was used.

Also researcher prepared computer based modules for teaching of values. To test its effectiveness Value Clarification Test was taken and t-test was used for analysis.

CHAPTER – 4
PRESENTATION OF DATA

In this chapter record sheets are presented which were used to identify the values from the supplementary reader book 'Lapwing' of English subject of standard – XII. There were twenty three reads in supplementary reader book 'Lapwing' of English subject of standard XII and first ten reads were taken. Therefore ten record sheets were prepared which are shown in this chapter. The various points of records are as describing.

1. Read number
2. Read name
3. Content of the Read
4. Reference sentences
5. Emerging value
6. Type of value
7. Learning Outcome
8. Remarks

RECORD SHEET - 1

READ – 1

THE BIRDMAN OF INDIA

There are many birds around us whether it's a city or a village. Most of us like watching colourful birds. However, there was a man who was so involved in their study that he was nicknamed 'The Birdman of India'. The name Dr.Salim Moizuddin Abdul Ali is synonymous with birds. He made birds a serious pursuit (attempt at achieving/gaining something) when it used to be mere fun for the most.

Orphaned (lost his parents) at a very young age, Salim Ali was brought up by his maternal Uncle. As a child Salim was given an expensive air gun as a present and spent all his time shooting sparrows around the house. One day he noticed that sparrows he had shot at had a yellow throat. He couldn't hold (was unable to stop) his curiosity and approached his uncle. His uncle who was equally clueless (no information/knowledge or idea of something) took him to the Bombay Natural History Society (BNHS) in the hope of finding an answer. There, the honorary secretary, W.S. Milliard told him that the bird was the Yellow Throated Sparrow. Milliard also told him about the variety of sparrows. That day Salim decided that he was going to be an ornithologist (a person who studies birds). No one would have imagined that the bird shooter would become a bird lover and nature conservator (a parson who protects values or things) one day!!

Inclination (desire/feeling that makes you work in a direction) and choice of a novel (new) career option made Salim's life full of hardship. As a young man Salim had to face years of unemployment. He moved to Burma to look after the family mining and timber business. It was a rewarding experience for the naturalist as there were endless opportunities for exploring the forests of Burma.

After returning to India, Salim tried to get a job as an ornithologist with the zoological Survey of India but was rejected since he did not have an M.sc or Ph.D. degree. He decided to study further to acquire eligibility (ability to do something /requirement) for the job. Salim went to Germany and got trained under Professor Stresemann, an acknowledged ornithologist in Berlin. However, when he came back to India he found out that there were still hardly any opportunities in his profession. Another man would have given up in disgust, but not Salim. He decided to create an opportunity. He went to the Bombay Natural History Society (BNHS) and offered his free services for conducting regional ornithological surveys.

Says Salim Ali, "It is seldom one gets an opportunity in life to do what one wants to do. I think the best results are those when you are doing something worthwhile which you enjoy doing without the motivation of material reward"

It was his sincerity that won him many awards and medals from all over the world including the Padma Shree and Padma Vibhusana.

Salim Ali was a true nature lover and his love for the wildlife is expressed in his autobiography (*The Fall of a Sparrow*) where he calls the wildlife a capital, an asset and says, "The interest on the capital must be used, while leaving the capital itself intact. This is how I interpret wildlife conservation and believe that future generation should enjoy the same fun with it that I had".

The Birdman is survived (*continued to live*) by his books on birds that a small group of people use to enjoy birding and endeavour for the conservation of the wildlife. Dr. Ali is no more but his legacy lives on.

Let's pay a tribute to the Birdman by leaning to identify a few birds around us. Before you start, study the names of different body parts of a bird given in the picture. It will help you understand the description as well as will enable you to describe birds.

The following are the descriptions of some common birds around us. Read the feature and try to notice them when you see them next.

1. White breasted Kingfisher: Size: Between Myna and Pigeon (28 cm). White throat and centre of breast, brown head and most of under parts. Seen at ponds, puddles, rain filled ditches, inundated (water covered) paddy fields and near seashore.

   Food : fish, tadpoles, lizards, grasshoppers and other insects.

   Nesting Season: March to July.

2. Indian Robin: Size: sparrow + (19 cm). A black bird with a white patch on wing. Reddish vent. Male has white shoulders and black under parts.

   Food: insets and their eggs, worms, spiders, etc. Nesting season: April to June.

3. Lora : Size : sparrow (14 cm). A black and yellow bird with two white wing bars. Male and female and better differentiated by a black tail. Crown and mantle of breeding males vary from uniformly black to black mixed with much yellow on mantle.

   Food : Insect, their eggs and larvae. Nesting season: Chiefly May to September.

4. Red-wattled Lapwing: Size: Partridge (Village Hen) (32-35 cm). Black cap and breast, red bill with black tip, and yellow legs.

   Food: insects, grubs, etc. Nesting Season : March to August. It is one of the rare birds that lay eggs on ground.

5. Paddy Bird/Pond Heron : Size: smaller than cattle egret (40-48 cm). Earthy brown in color when at rest but with the glistening white wing, tail and rump flashing when it flies. Food: Frogs, fish, crabs and insects. Nesting Season: May to September.

6. River Tern: Size : Crow size (38-46 cm). Orange yellow bill, black cap, grayish white under parts.

   Food : Fish, prawns, swimming crabs. Nesting Season : May-June

7. Bronze-winged Jacana : Size : Equivalent to village hen (
    28 -31 cm). Dark upper—wing and under-wing, bronze
    green upper part and blackish under part.

    Food : Seeds, roots , etc. Nesting Season : June to
    September.

8. Indian Roller/Blue Jay : Size : Pigeon (33 cm). Rufous-
    brown on nape (back of neck) and under parts, white
    streaking on ear-coverts and throat, and greenish mantle.

    Food : Insects Nesting Season : February to March

Reference Sentence – 1

One day he noticed that sparrows he had shot at had a
yellow throat. He couldn't hold (was unable to stop) his
curiosity and approached his uncle.

Emerging Value

Curiosity

Type of Value

Personal Value

Learning Outcome

Healthy curiosity is a great key in innovation.

Remarks

Reference Sentence – 2

He decided to study further to acquire eligibility
(ability to do something /requirement) for the job. Salim

went to Germany and got trained under Professor Stresemann, an acknowledged ornithologist in Berlin.

Emerging Value

Quest for Knowledge

Type of Value

Spiritual Value

Learning Outcome

The greatest enemy of knowledge is not ignorance; it is the illusion of knowledge.

Remarks

Reference Sentence – 3

He went to the Bombay Natural History Society (BNHS) and offered his free services for conducting regional ornithological surveys.

Emerging Value

Helpfulness

Type of Value

Personal Value

Learning Outcome

Show goodness onto the world and the world will show goodness onto you.

Remarks

Reference Sentence – 4

It was his sincerity that won him many awards and medals from all over the world including the Padma Shree and Padma Vibhusana.

Emerging Value

Dignity of the Individual

Type of Value

Social Value

Learning Outcome

When it comes to human dignity, we cannot make compromises.

Remarks

Reference Sentence – 5

Let's pay a tribute to the Birdman by leaning to identify a few birds around us.

Emerging Value

Gratitude

Type of Value

Personal Value

Learning Outcome

Let us be grateful to the people who make us happy; they are the charming gardeners who make our souls blossom.

Remarks

Reference Sentence – 6

Salim Ali was a true nature lover and his love for the wildlife is expressed in his autobiography (*The Fall of a Sparrow*) where he calls the wildlife a capital, an asset and says,

Emerging Value

Kindness to Animals

Type of Value

Social Value

Learning Outcome

We should protect wild life.

Remarks

RECORD SHEET - 2

READ – 2

HER WORDS, HIS VISION

One afternoon while waiting for her husband to finish a business meeting, Mansi toured (visited) an art museum. She was looking forward to a quiet view of the masterpieces.

A young couple is viewing the paintings ahead of her chattered (kept talking) nonstop between themselves. She observed them a moment and found the lady only talking all the time. Mansi thought of the man and admired his patience for putting up with her constant parade of words.

Mansi gazed at (kept looking) them several times as she moved through the various rooms of art. Each time she heard the lady's constant gush of words, she moved away quickly.

Mansi was standing at the counter of the museum gift shop making purchase when the couple approached the exit. Mansi observed the couple carefully. The man after paying the bill pulled out a white stick and tapped his way towards the gate.

"He's a brave man". The clerk at the counter said." Most of us would give up if we were blinded at such a young age. During his recovery, he made a vow that his life wouldn't change. So, as before, he and his wife come in whenever there's a new art show".

"But what does he get out of the art ?" Mansi asked " He can't see".

"Can't see ! You are wrong. He sees a lot. More than you or I do," the clerk said. " his wife describes each painting through his mind's eye. So he can see."

Mansi learned something about patience, courage and love, that day. She saw the patience of young wife describing paintings to a person without sight and the courage of a husband who would not allow blindness to alter his life.

Mansi witnessed the love shared by the two people as she watched this couple walk away with their arms interwined. "Really her words are his vision" said Mansi.

Reference Sentence – 1

Mansi thought of the man and admired his patience for putting up with her constant parade of words.

Emerging Value

Patience

Type of Value

Moral Value

Learning Outcome

Patience is bitter, but its fruit is sweet.

Remarks

Reference Sentence – 2

Mansi gazed at (kept looking) them several times as she moved through the various rooms of art.

Emerging Value

Curiosity

Type of Value

Personal Value

Learning Outcome

Healthy curiosity is a great key in innovation.

Remarks

Reference Sentence – 3

"He's a brave man". The clerk at the counter said." Most of us would give up if we were blinded at such a young age.

Emerging Value

Courage

Type of Value

Personal Value

Learning Outcome

Courage is unconquered army.

Remarks

Reference Sentence – 4

"His wife describes each painting through his mind's eye. So he can see."

Emerging Value

Consideration for others

Type of Value

Personal Value

Learning Outcome

Good works is giving to the poor and the helpless, but divine works is showing them their worth to the One who matters.

Remarks

Reference Sentence – 5

She saw the patience of young wife describing paintings to a person without sight and the courage of a husband who would not allow blindness to alter his life.

Emerging Value

Self-respect

Type of Value

Personal Value

Learning Outcome

Respect yourself and others will respect you.

Remarks

Reference Sentence – 6

Mansi witnessed the love shared by the two people as she watched this couple walk away with their arms intertwined.

Emerging Value

Compassion

Type of Value

Social Value

Learning Outcome

Love and compassion are necessities, not luxuries. Without them, humanity cannot survive.

Remarks

RECORD SHEET - 3

READ – 3

FINAL GAME

Before the final game, life was ordinary, daily routine. Each day I awakened with a mental list of tasks I had to complete before the end of the day. My life wasn't too complicated: class, soccer (football) practice, studying and sleep. Often 1 returned home from soccer field after heavy practice to study until the early of the morning.

Having accepted well to daily routine, I never imagined it would be altered. However, my life changed the day on the final game. It was the last game of the tournament; and winner would achieve 'championship'. My team had been under vigorous (tough) physical training for the past four years in anticipation of this day. But emotionally we were ready as well. I was ready. I entered the game with the mindset that the title was in our hands. We deserved it because our desire to win was great!

"Captains!" called the referee. I approached the centre of the field, and with confidence, looked in the eyes of my opponent while giving her a powerful handshake, wishing her luck. As I took my position on the field, I knew it was time for the final game to begin. I took a deep breath and reassured myself that I would give this game best of my abilities as if it were the last game I ever played.

"Goalie, Goalie" called the man dressed in black and white. The two goalies simultaneously raised their right hands in air, indicating that they were ready. The game could begin. This was it. The whistle sounded, and the ball was soon kicked in my direction. I received the ball and kicked it twenty feet toward the goal just in time for my teammate to meet it and pound (strike, hit) it right into the net. "Goal" everyone shouted. The game had started out well.

But the power of the game soon grew intense as the opposing team came right back at us with a goal to tie the game at one to one. The game continued at the extremely competitive level throughout the first half and into the second. The score was still tied at one to one until I received the ball with one minute to go. I needed to put the ball in the net, and I did just that, making the final score two to one. But it didn't go exactly as planned.

In an attempt to block my shot, my opponent challenged me in midair. But instead of heading the ball, her body slammed into mine leaving me unconscious in the middle of the field. My teammates shouted cries of victory and horror at the same time.

When I regained consciousness, I found myself in a hospital bed, surrounded by family, friends and teammates. Also at my side were doctors, the determiners of my future. In a matter of moments, they would tell me the severity of my injuries.

I was told that I would have to undergo an extremely rarer surgery. This type of surgery had only been performed a limited number of times, with a mere 50 percent success rate. After some thinking, I decided to undergo the surgery, knowing that either way, many challenges would await me. Would I be able to finish my studies? What effect would it have on my social life, my grades? These question circled my head, and unfortunately, only time would provide answers.

After the surgery, I was no longer the independent person as before. I had to depend on other to assist me in even the simplest tasks. It was going to be a long tough road to recovery, and I knew I couldn't get through it without a positive attitude. Gradually I cloud adjust to the changes in my life. I began to realize that I didn't have to give up my old life completely and I focused my energy on a favourite pastime: writing. I was able to produce work of art in the in the silence and solace of my mind and spirit. Although I was not in physical control of half of my body, I still had control of my mind.

Looking back on the situation as a whole I am glad that the final game was, in fact, my final game. I have no regrets. I said "I would give it best of my abilities and I did that and ultimately, I came out a winner." Although my accident robbed me of my physical abilities, it left me with power of mind and forced me to discover my inner self. That final game was more rewarding. Not only did we win, but I was able to discover a new level within. I guess I gained two victories that day.

Reference Sentence – 1

Often I returned home from soccer field after heavy practice to study until the early of the morning.

Emerging Value

Self-Study

Type of Value

Personal Value

Learning Outcome

Self-study leads to self-development and self-liberation.

Remarks

Reference Sentence – 2

My team had been under vigorous (tough) physical training for the past four years in anticipation of this day.

Emerging Value

Dignity of Manual Work

Type of Value

Social Value

Learning Outcome

The three great essentials to achieve anything worthwhile are, first, hard work; second, stick-to-itiveness; third, common sense.

Remarks

Reference Sentence – 3

I entered the game with the mind-set that the title was in our hands.

Emerging Value

Self-confidence

Type of Value

Personal Value

Learning Outcome

One important key to success is self-confidence. An important key to self-confidence is preparation.

Remarks

Reference Sentence – 4

We deserved it because our desire to win was great!

Emerging Value

Team-work

Type of Value

Moral Value

Learning Outcome

Teamwork divides the task and multiplies the success

Remarks

Reference Sentence – 5

I took a deep breath and reassured myself that I would give this game best of my abilities as if it were the last game I ever played.

Emerging Value

Self-help

Type of Value

Personal Value

Learning Outcome

You are essentially who you create yourself to be and all that occurs in your life is the result of your own making.

Remarks

Reference Sentence – 6

The score was still tied at one to one until I received the ball with one minute to go. I needed to put the ball in the net, and I did just that, making the final score two to one. But it didn't go exactly as planned.

Emerging Values :

Curiosity

Type of Value

Personal Value

Learning Outcome

Curiosity is one of the permanent and certain characteristics of a vigorous mind.

Remarks

Reference Sentence – 7

I found myself in a hospital bed, surrounded by family, friends and teammates.

Emerging Value

Friendship

Type of Value

Social Value

Learning Outcome

Friend in need is a friend indeed.

Remarks

Reference Sentence – 8

Not only did we win, but I was able to discover a new level within. I guess I gained two victories that day.

Emerging Value

Self-control

Type of Value

Personal Value

Learning Outcome

Self-control is the chief element in self-respect, and self-respect is the chief element in courage.

Remarks

RECORD SHEET - 4

READ – 4

I LOVE ME

Hello,   I'm Swayam Saxene…

When I was younger, I was very shy. Whenever I even thought of speaking to new people about anything, my whole head would turn red. I'm sure people could even see me withdrawn from behind my back.

By the time I reached high school, I was so stressed out by the thought of answering questions and doing group projects that my self-confidence problem would get in the way of my ability to study.

I was nervous and agitated about being wrong and how people would react to me. My school and work started to suffer. Because of my inferiority complex, I couldn't go out. I was afraid of even going for shopping. I couldn't speak to people or make decisions. I hid myself away and felt like a real loser.

That's when my negativity made me upset. There was nothing that I didn't over analyse and criticise. The combination of my self-criticism, low self-confidence and bad self-image was staring to destroy the life I wanted to build for myself.

I had to conquer (overcome) my low self-esteem (love for the self). I had no other option.

One day I made a decision to change, and I started to read everything I could about self-help.

I wanted to be a speaker and an author. Seems odd, I know, but it was my lifelong dream. I saw other people standing up, making a difference, and doing it with an ease that I couldn't even fathom (understand).

Why was it so difficult for me? I realized then that I needed to:

Understand exactly why I felt low.

- Figure out why I was thinking everything as negative - The way people looked at me, their comments, their actions… it was literally destroying me.

- Understand how much harm I was causing myself

- Find effective ways to pause, recognize my negative behaviour, and eliminate (remove, get rid of) the obstacles I was creating for my self - I was the only one with the power to do it.

The Results…

Once I discovered the techniques that worked for me, my confidence grew and I began to see challenges as opportunities to move forward and succeed.

Now I enjoy meeting people and my relationships are much better. I have more friends and can rely on them when I feel myself slipping back to where I was before.

I am achieving my goals with ease because I have developed my self-confidence.

I no longer miss the opportunities that life offers. I am more optimistic and my mind no longer limits me.

Life is finally good!

Here are some strategies for building love for one's own self:

- Free yourself from "should've". Live your life on the basis of what is possible for you and what feels right to you instead of what you or others think you "should" do. Find out what you want and what you are good at.

- Respect your own needs. Respecting your deeper needs will increase your sense of worth and well-doing.

- Set achievable goals. Establish goals on the basis of what you can realistically achieve, and then work step-by-step to develop your strength.

- Talk to yourself positively. When you notice that you are doubting or judging yourself, replace such thoughts with self-supportive direction.

- Seek out and put yourself in situations in which the probability of success is high.

- Take chances. New experiences are learning experiences which can build self-confidence. Expect to make mistakes as part of the process; don't be disappointed if you don't do it perfectly. Feet good about trying something new, making progress and increasing your competence.

- Solve problems. Don't avoid problems. Face them, and identify ways to solve them or cope with them.

- Make decisions. Trust yourself to deal with the results.
- Develop your skills. Know what you can and can't do.
- Focus on what you can do rather than what you cannot.

Reference Sentence – 1

The combination of my self-criticism, low self-confidence and bad self-image was staring to destroy the life I wanted to build for myself.

Emerging Value

Initiative

Type of Value

Personal Value

Learning Outcome

Initiative is the first step towards success.

Remarks

Reference Sentence – 2

I had to conquer (overcome) my low self-esteem (love for the self). I had no other option.

Emerging Value

Self-respect

Type of Value

Personal Value

Learning Outcome

Self-respect is the root of discipline.

Remarks

Reference Sentence – 3

One day I made a decision to change, and I started to read everything I could about self-help.

Emerging Value

Self-help

Type of Value

Personal Value

Learning Outcome

Always be fearless. Walk like lion, talk like pigeons, live like elephants and love like an infant child.

Remarks

Reference Sentence – 4

My confidence grew and I began to see challenges as opportunities to move forward and succeed.

Emerging Value

Self-confidence

Type of Value

Personal Value

Learning Outcome

Believe you can and you're halfway there.

Remarks

Reference Sentence – 5

I have more friends and can rely on them when I feel myself slipping back to where I was before.

Emerging Value

Friendship

Type of Value

Social Value

Learning Outcome

Best friend is one who bring outs best in ones.

Remarks

RECORD SHEET - 5

READ – 5

PENCIL

My daughter,

Little dear daughter,

Lights a pencil

With a sharpener.

The sky of the white paper

Begins to be filled with light.

The black bird flying away with

the tree;

Glasses on the eyes of the

peacock;

The fire-chariot flying in the air;

The airplane walking on the

road;

The lion having a conversation

with the cow;

A one - eyes sun on the black tree

With a patch of cloud over it;

A blue fish flying on the

forehead of the loud;

The yellow butterfly swimming

in the waterfall

My darling daughter,

In her ecstasy,

Is busy drawing

Strange pictures.

But when the schoolmaster

Gives her homework,

My darling doll

Breaks the tip of the pencil

In anger,

And the candle of the pencil

is extinguished

Only the smoke remains

On the sky of the while paper.

Reference Sentence – 1

My darling daughter,

In her ecstasy,

Is busy drawing

Strange pictures.

Emerging Value

Ecstasy

Type of Value

Spiritual Value

Learning Outcome

The highest ecstasy is the attention at its fullest.

Remarks

RECORD SHEET - 6

READ – 6

1. I Miss You, Mother

Early in the autumn of 1984, my mother began writing the story of her life. She was an energetic woman in her seventies. It was her desire to put down her thoughts and memories in her "My Book". Once she came for dinner and told me that she had to work on her book. I laughed and asked her where the fire was. The fire was inside her. She finished her book in early December. Three days after Christmas, her cancer was discovered and three months later she was dead.

From my Mother's book:

I have loved family friends, nature, animals, music and many other things. It will be hard to say good bye to those I love and to the beauty in the world.

I read these words for the first time when I was surrounded by packing boxes in my mother's apartment, a month after her death. I tried to picture her face as I read the words but the memories of the last two months as she lay dying, were too painful. I closed her book.

On a rainy sunday afternoon, one year from the day my mother was admitted to the hospital. I suddenly knew the time had come to remember and honour her life and her death. For a month I kept on reading the notebook I had kept during her hospitalization and my mother's book. When I finished reading. I realized that my mother was no longer lost to me; in some new and different way I had regained her.

From my notes, dated January 21, 1985.

My mother continues to amaze me. Despite what is happening to her body, she continues to appreciate nature and the small bit of life. Her room no. 235 has a large window. She enjoys watching birds busily flying outside.

Her pain is awesome (severe). She can no longer sit up. Today is her grandson's birthday, and somehow she managed to write a note to him. One day I will tell him of the unimaginable amount of effort his grandmother put into writing this note.

One warm day is February, I opened the window in her room. The soft, scented air spilled in. My mother opened her eyes and asked," is the grass beginning to grow?"

I closed my eyes and stream of memory ran across.

From my diary when I was five years old:

I have stepped out of the house in the middle of a summer night to watch the grass and flowers in our garden. Suddenly my mother is at my side. Instead of sending me back to bed, she joins me, we sit there together. Listening to the noise made by cicadas (a type of insect). "Look" she says, pointing to a shooting star. But I am looking at the light in her eyes. Later I fall asleep with my head in her lap.

I remember the day my mother asked that I write a last message from her to each member of the family. I wrote through my tears. I was aware that while my mother has accepted her death, I hadn't. Over the next few days, my mother wanted to talk about her life so we began our long, final conversation. As we walked, the picture of my mother's life grew stronger.

From my mother's book:

I haven't forgotten what it's like to be young-all the hopes and anxieties and the sensation in everything you do is going to advance or wreck your life. No in between when you are young.

My ambition was to go on a stage. My sister and I took dancing lessons and practiced difficult steps. In those days I thought I'd be a famous actress! It was all a dream of course.

Lying in the hospital, my mother had other dreams. One morning she awoke, and told me of her dream. She had seen a man fall from a roof. All that day her thoughts were of falling.

"Don't be afraid" I reassured her." Of course, I will catch you. For all those years when I was growing up, you caught me. Now it's my turn."

Her face relaxed under the oxygen mask. But I knew there would come a time- and soon – when I would have to let her go.

And so would she.

From my notes, March 1, 1985.

She is very weak and her breathing is irregular. But her spirit is still connected to the world. When I held the pot of flowers close to her, she said delightedly," Oh' that's so pretty! I isn't it wonderful how life goes on?"

That next to last evening of my mother's life, she stared out of the window into the blackness.

"What are you looking at?" I asked her.

"Nothing." She replied.

"Well" I said, "Look at me."

More than anything else I wanted her last moments more than anything else. I wanted them to be spent looking at the face of someone who loved her.

The summer after my mother died, when the first yellow lily appeared, I ran into the house to telephone my mother with the news. Then I remembered that she is no more. Even now, I keep thinking of things I ought to tell her, things I want to ask her. She had a way of giving perspective to my life.

From my mother's book

When I turned seventy, someone asked me how it felt to have arrived at such an age well even though my body isn't the same, I am still the same. I will always be the girl who loved cats and flowers and raced home from school to practice my dancing lessons. Inside I am still that person.

I miss that person.

Reference Sentence – 1

I have loved family friends, nature, animals, music and many other things.

Emerging Value

Universal Love

Type of Value

Global Value

Learning Outcome

When the element of hatred is someday universally replaced with love and kindness, humanity will see peace.

Remarks

Reference Sentence – 2

She continues to appreciate nature and the small bit of life.

Emerging Value

Kindness to Animals

Type of Value

Social Value

Learning Outcome

We should protect wild life.

Remarks

READ – 7

2. The Princess and The Tiger

There was once a king. If anyone committed a serious crime in the kingdom, the king did not condemn (give punishment) him to death. Instead the criminal would be taken to a large arena (a place for public events). All the people would come to see the show. In the arena there were two doors. Behind one door there was a fierce and hungry tiger. Behind the other there was a beautiful young girl. The man would not know which door was which. He would have to choose one of the two doors. If he chose well, he had to marry the girl. If he chose badly…..the tiger would eat him.

The king had a very beautiful daughter. One day he found out that she had fallen in love with a poor young soldier in his army. The king was very angry. The soldier was arrested and taken to the arena.

The princess knew which door concealed (hid) the tiger and which one concealed the beautiful girl. However, she was a very jealous princess and did not want the soldier to marry the girl behind the door. Neither did she want to see her lover killed by the tiger.

When the soldier was brought into the arena he looked up and saw the princess sitting next to her father.

What signal do you think she made to the soldier? And what happened to the soldier in the end?

Reference Sentence – 1

There was once a king. If anyone committed a serious crime in the kingdom, the king did not condemn (give punishment) him to death.

Emerging Value

Justice

Type of Value

Social Value

Learning Outcome

Justice delayed is Justice denied.

Remarks

Reference Sentence – 2

The king had a very beautiful daughter. One day he found out that she had fallen in love with a poor young soldier in his army.

Emerging Value

Love

Type of Value

Personal Value

Learning Outcome

Love is usually wonderful.

Remarks

READ – 8

3. Ananya Writes to His Parents

Dear mummy, Dear Pappa

I love you both.

Yesterday I saw a child on a merry go round. He waved at his parents every round. The parents waved back too. The incident ran through my mind the whole day and I kept asking a question to myself: 'Where do the parents get patience from to express love for their child in trivial (small) activities of life?' for searching the answer, I went back to my childhood and realized that on each day of your life, you made deposits in the memory banks of your children. In bringing me and Asmi up, you had built self-esteem first and our house later. You had finger-paint (painting the fingers) more and pointed the finger less. You had done less correcting but more connecting. You had run through more fields and gazed at more stars for us.

Today I am just crossing the border between my childhood and adulthood. I am no longer a child now. In these years of my adolescence, I have unlimited confusions. I have started feeling that 'growing up' is quite scary, whereas being a 'grown up' has many attractions. The responsibilities that go with growing age often come as surprise. I think now I have started developing an understanding about why and how you did what for us.

For last several years, I have been talking about my freedom. I remember the day when you objected to my dress and hair. That day you appeared to me like an evil dictators (absolute rulers), who would never understand my style, my personality. The next day you did not allow me to go out. I was fiercely angry on you. We were on opposite sides and there seemed no meeting grounds. Now, when I recall this incident, I also remember how you appreciated (praised) my choice when we had to buy a gift for Asmi. I also recall how after getting angry on me for the bad report card for a few hours, both of you came into my room and explained what I should do to score more marks. I have both the types of memory but now I would prefer to remember the best. The little and big mishaps between us were just thoughtless reactions.

I need you both to be with me and understand me about my decisions regarding what's wrong and what's right. I wish to try out my ways to deal with the situation around me. I recall that when I was learning to walk, I used to fall quite often. But with your love and care, I learnt to get up and run. While experimenting in my life I know, I may fail, but I am also sure that you will be there with me. I have learnt from you that experience generates strength to begin anew after committing mistakes.

I have seen you both and Asmi argue over what she should become. Mummy…Pappa, I know, you have a right to suggest what fits her personality the best. But as 'understanding persons' let us respect her feelings and her wishes. Our over aspirations might suffocate her growth. You might disagree to what I think.

But this is what I feel and think. I hope you also want Asmi to venture on the path of life with her own maturity. Trust in her abilities and a little encouragement will facilitate her to learn how to respond to changing situations.

Reading this, you must be feeling that your Ananya has really become `a man'. Yes, I have grown up. You both have contributed to my 'understanding'. I love you both for your wise, timely counsel (advise) and friendly attitude. I am sure we will live as a happy family 'forever'.

Your loving son,

Ananya

Reference Sentence – 1

In bringing me and Asmi up, you had built self-esteem first and our house later. You had finger-painted (painting the fingers) more and pointed the finger less.

Emerging Value

Self-respect

Type of Value

Personal Value

Learning Outcome

We cannot conceive of a greater loss than the loss of one's self-respect.

Remarks

Reference Sentence – 2

For last several years, I have been talking about my freedom.

Emerging Value

Freedom

Type of Value

Political Value

Learning Outcome

Those who deny freedom to others deserve it not for themselves.

Remarks

Reference Sentence – 3

I need you both to be with me and understand me about my decisions regarding what's wrong and what's right. I wish to try out my ways to deal with the situation around me.

Emerging Value

Common Good

Type of Value

Social Value

Learning Outcome

We need to rediscover the idea of the common good and work together to build a happy world.

Remarks

Reference Sentence – 4

Mummy…Pappa, I know, you have a right to suggest what fits her personality the best. But as 'understanding persons' let us respect her feelings and her wishes.

Emerging Value

Consideration for Others

Type of Value

Personal Value

Learning Outcome

Power is the ability to do good things for others.

Remarks

Reference Sentence – 5

I hope you also want Asmi to venture on the path of life with her own maturity. Trust in her abilities and a little encouragement will facilitate her to learn how to respond to changing situations.

Emerging Value

Faithfulness

Type of Value

Personal Value

Learning Outcome

We should be faithful to our country.

Remarks

Reference Sentence – 6

You both have contributed to my 'understanding'. I love you both for your wise, timely counsel (advise) and friendly attitude. I am sure we will live as a happy family 'forever'.

Emerging Value

Respect for Others

Type of Value

Moral Value

Learning Outcome

Everyone should be respected as an individual, but no one idolized.

Remarks

____

4. Vismay @ Search

It is almost a week now. Vismay, a bright, ambitious and hardworking student of 12th science looks confused to his class teacher. One day during the recess, the teacher sat for lunch with. Vismay and asked, "You are hardworking and scoring very well in all the subjects then way are you so mush worried over something? If you have any problem you can share it with me."

Vismay didn't speak for a while. He was staring at a tree outside the window. The teacher held Vismay by his shoulder and said," Feel free, and do not hesitate. Every problem has a solution."

Vismay took a deep breath and said," Actually…. I am thinking about my studies after 12th. I don't know much about aeronautics but I want to know more about it and wish to join the course somewhere. But….I….don't know anything about a college that offers such course."

"Is this the reason..!!!" , exclaimed the teacher . "Thanks to the internet. It's not at all a problem now. Come with me. Within half an hour, you will be free from your worries. By the way, do you have an access to the internet?"

I access the net for e-mail only."

"That's good. You will be able to understand quickly then."

After the lunch, the teacher took Vishay to the computer lab, logged on to the internet and said, "Here you are!!Read this…it gives all information on what is aeronautical engineering."

"Its' so fast….. How did you do it within no time, Sir? Can I get information on anything? Can I also know about institutions that offer courses in aeronautical engineering?" Vishay was exited.

"Yes, my boy…with the help of Search Engines, you need not depend on libraries or any other source for getting information."

"What is this Search Engine?" asked Vismay.

"A web Search Engine is a tool designed to search for information on the World Wide Web. All you need to do is to enter a word or a phrase in the search engine and it will display the list of websites in which the word/phrase occurs", replied the teacher.

"Is it difficult to use a search engine?"

"Not at all… All you need to know is how to make your search effective as the internet has piles of information. You need to learn three simple steps to do it. Let me show you how to search!!!

Step one: Identify the Keyword/phrase

Decide what you to search for and prepare a list of keywords or phrases that will describe what to search for before you log on to the internet.

For example, you want to know institutes or colleges that offer aeronautical engineering, isn't it? So for that our key phrase will be:

Institute of aeronautical engineering

This will give you a list of websites that have the words ''institute'', ''aeronautical'' and ''engineering'' in them. It would be a very beg list. If you want to limit your search, you can put your phrase in toll. For example,

"Institute of aeronautical engineering"

It will search for the websites that have exactly the same phrase or sentence in it.

Step two: Start Searching

Once the list is ready, log on to the net, go to any search engine and enter the keyword or phrase in the search box, click on 'Search' button and your search will begin.

Tips for entering the keyword:

1. Search is always case insensitive. Searching for [solar system] is same as searching for [solar system].

2. With some exceptions, punctuation is ignored. You can't Search for @#$ %^&*() =+ []/and other special characters.

3. Always use a group of words while searching instead of a single word. This will help you get focused results.

4. When you want to use two or more phrases during Search use the + sing. Example: grammar + exercise or preposition + exercise. This will Search for the sites that have both grammar/preposition and exercise in them.

5. If your keyword is a phrase and you want to Search for websites that have the exact phrase in it, then add quotation marks ""and a plus sing. Example: "+English Language Teaching".

Step Three: Narrow down the Search

After entering the keywords and getting the results for the Search, you can use the Search within Results option to narrow down on the sites you are interested in. Scroll down the page and go to Search within Results option. For example, you may specify the city of your choice by entering name in the Search within Results box.

1. The Title: The first line of any search result is the title of the webpage.

2. The Snippet: A description of or an excerpt from the webpage.

3. The URL: The webpage's address.

4. Cached link: A link to an earlier version of this page. Click here if the page you wanted isn't available.

I am sure you will learn as you start using search engines. Experience is the best teacher. There are many more things to learn but own your own. I think the best way to start is to start searching additional information on your textbook topics. So, start using search engines and keep yourself updated and abreast of the new information. Dear Vishay, internet is full of information on almost all subjects. What you need to have is curiosity. All the best!! "

Reference Sentence – 1

"You are hard-working and scoring very well in all the subjects then way are you so much worried over something? If you have any problem you can share it with me."

Emerging Value

Co-Operation

Type of Value

Social Value

Learning Outcome

If you want to be incrementally better: Be competitive. If you want to be exponentially better: Be cooperative.

Remarks

Reference Sentence – 2

"Thanks to the internet. It's not at all a problem now. Come with me. Within half an hour, you will be free from your worries. By the way, do you have an access to the internet?"

Emerging Value

Quest for Knowledge

Type of Value

Spiritual Value

Learning Outcome

An investment in knowledge always pays the best interest.

Remarks

---

5. The Blind Boy

O say what is that thing call'd light,

Which I must ne'er enjoy;

What are the blessings of the sight,

O tell your poor blind boy!

You talk of wondrous things you see,

You say the sun shines bright;

I feel him warm, but how can he

Or make it day or night?

My day or night myself I make

Whene'er I sleep or play;

And could I ever keep awake

With heavy sighs I often hear

With heavy sighs I often hear

You mourn your hapless woe;

But sure with patience I can bear

A loss I ne'er can know.

Then let not what I cannot have

My cheer of mind destroy:

Whilst thus I sing, I am a king,

Although a poor blind boy.

Reference Sentence – 1

You say the sun shines bright;

I feel him warm, but how can he

Or make it day or night?

Emerging Value

Self-Reliable

Type of Value

Personal Value

Learning Outcome

Trust your instincts, and make judgements on what your heart tells you. The heart will not betray you.

Remarks

Reference Sentence – 2

With heavy sighs I often hear

You mourn your hapless woe;

But sure with patience I can bear

A loss I ne'er can know.

Emerging Value

Patience

Type of Value

Personal Value

Learning Outcome

Patience is a conquering virtue.

Remarks

Reference Sentence – 3

Then let not what I cannot have

My cheer of mind destroy:

Whilst thus I sing, I am a king,

Although a poor blind boy.

Emerging Value

Faithfulness

Type of Value

Personal Value

Learning Outcome

Nothing is nobler than faithfulness.

Remarks

CHAPTER - 5
CONSTRUCTION OF COMPUTER BASED MODULES

5.1 INTRODUCTION

In the present research, computer based modules for teaching of values was prepared. For this movie maker software was used.

5.2 CONSTRUCTION OF COMPUTER BASED MODULES

Various steps which were given by Ambasana (2002) for computer based program were followed.

5.2.1 Selection of Subject and Reads.

In this step subject and Reads for preparing computer based modules were selected. English subject was selected and four reads were selected which were (1) The Birdman of India, (2) Her Words, His Vision (3) Final Game (4) I Love me.

Sub topics and values derived from each Read were as describing.

Read – 1 : The Birdman of India
Values
1. Curiosity 2. Quest for Knowledge 3. Helpfulness 4. Dignity of the Individual 5. Kindness to animals 6. Gratitude
Read – 2 : Her Words, His Vision
Values
1. Patience 2. Curiosity 3. Courage 4. Consideration for others 5. Self-respect 6. Compassion
Read – 3 : Final Game
Values
1. Self-Study 2. Dignity of Manual Work

3. Self-confidence
4. Team-work
5. Self-help
6. Curiosity
7. Friendship
8. Self-control
Read – 4 : I Love Me
Values
1. Initiative 2. Self-respect 3. Self-help 4. Self-confidence 5. Friendship

5.2.2 Formulation of Objectives

After selecting subject and Read's objective of computer based modules were formulated, which are as describing.

Read – 1 : The Birdman of India

- To know about Dr Salim Moizuddin Abdul Ali

- To know about Various birds.

- To know about an ornithologist's life.

- To get familiar with Salim Ali and his work.

- To know about curiosity.

- To know about quest for knowledge.

- To know about gratitude.

- To know about dignity of the individual.

- To Know about kindness to animals.

Read – 2 : Her Words, His Vision

- To know about Mansi's views.

- To know about chattered young couple.

- To know about patience.

- To know about consideration for others.

- To know about courage.

- To know about self-respect

- To know about compassion.

Read – 3 : Final Game

- To Know about game of soccer.

- To know about self-study.

- To know about dignity of manual work.

- To know about curiosity.

- To know about team work.

- To know about self - confidence.

- To know about friendship.

- To know about self-help.

- To know about self-control.

Read – 4 : I Love Me

- To Know about Swayam Saxena's character.

- To know about initiative.

- To know about self-respect.

- To know about self-help.

- To know about self - confidence.

- To know about friendship.

5.2.3   Formation of Story Board

The process of arranging the content in logical sequence, in written or non-written form is called story board. Keeping content and values in mind the story board was prepared in this chapter. The opinion of experts was taken. Expert's request letter was given in appendix – V and expert's name were given in appendix – VI. After taking the expert opinion, final story board was prepared.

5.2.4 Formation of files of written content

In the present research the written information was typed in MS WORD in Times New Roman fonts. This file of MS WORD was saved in the folder which was named, content.

5.2.5 Formation of graphic folder

In the present research content was presented along with pictures. For this image search option of, www.google.co.in was used. Pictures related to content, values and maps were downloaded and saved in the graphic folder.

5.2.6 Formation of video folder

In the present research relevant videos were also presented along with. For this video search option of, www.youtube.com was used. Videos related to content and values were downloaded and saved in the video folder.

5.2.7 Formation of audio folder

In the present research sound files were also downloaded. For this, www.youtube.com, www.clip.dj.com websites were was used. Sound files related to content and values were downloaded and saved in the audio folder.

5.3 ABOUT MOVIE MAKER

Movie Maker is a software which is used to prepare short movies from photographs and videos. This software by Microsoft Corporation comes along with windows operating system like windows 2003, windows xp, windows 2007 etc. This main advantage of this software is that it is very user friendly. After adding photos and videos one can also add audio in the movie. Captions can be added on photo and video also. Also the facility of voice recording and slide timings is also available in movie maker. The work in movie maker was saved as movie maker project with the extension of .wlmp. After the project is completed movie was saved in mp4 format. This software is very useful for preparing Educational Programs. Menu bar of the Movie Maker Software is as under;

> Put photos
>
> File extension
>
> Movie saving options
>
> Extension of movie.

5.3.1 Preparation of computer based modules

Keeping in mind the content and values, computer based modules were prepared. The steps for preparation of computer based modules are as describing.

1. Based on the values emerging from four Reads', small videos, songs, slide show, photographs, cartoon, animated movie etc. were downloaded, edited and kept in video folder.

2. Then the whole content of all the Reads were typed in MS WORD.

3. In Power Point appropriate slide background and font colour were selected. Content of text book from MS

WORD was copied to slides. Content was copied with appropriate font size and quantity of text in a slide.

4. Reference sentences were highlighted and emerging values were shown. After that slides of meaning and understanding of values were prepared and then small story, photographs, for that particular value was added.

5. Then all slides were converted and saved in the photographic form with the extension of .jpeg, with the help of save as options.

6. In Movie Maker above photos were imported and arranged.

7. For each slide voice recording was done using narration tool.

8. Then videos, cartoon movies, animated movies related to values were added.

9. Then the Movie Maker project was saved in .wlmp file.

10. From file option the project was saved from save as mp4 movie.

5.4 PRIMARY PRE-PILOTING OF COMPUTER BASED MODULES

After preparing any computer based modules pre-piloting is necessary. In pre-piloting expert opinions, teachers opinions and students responses were obtained.

1. **Experts' opinion.** After preparation of modules expert opinions were taken. Opinions were obtained mainly in slide format, slide background, font size, content in one

slide, design, animation etc. Also changes were made according to experts' opinion.

2. **Teachers' opinion.** Opinions of teachers were also taken. Opinions were obtained from them mainly in content of text, logical sequence of content, addition of photos and maps etc. Changes were made according to the experts' opinion.

3. **Students' Opinion.** Pre-piloting was done on small group of students and responses were collected. Based on pre-piloting method of explaining content in simple form, concentration of students, way of delivering content, timings of each slide, etc. were changed for better understanding of students.

5.5 CONSTRUCTION OF FINAL MODULES

After experts' opinions, teachers' opinions and students' responses, necessary changes were incorporated and final computer based modules were prepared.

5.6 IMPLEMENTATION OF EXPERIMENT

5.6.1 Introduction

The chief aim of experiment is to test the effectiveness of independent variable on dependent variable. As an independent variable computer based modules and as dependent variable difference between value score of Value Clarification Test was taken. It was to examine that if using computer based modules value score can be affected or not.

For this the researcher had selected Shree M.B. Ajmera High School, Vinchhiya by convenience method. Permission was taken from Principal regarding the experiment.

5.6.2   Implementation

Experiment was conducted in four stages, which are also known as characteristics of experiment. Characteristic of experiment: (1) control (2) manipulation (3) observation (4) replication.

1.   **Control.** Variables that are not of direct interest to the researcher, called extraneous variable, need to be controlled. In the present study variables which were controlled were: school, standard, subject, content matter, medium of study, and learning environment.

2.   **Manipulation.** Manipulation refers to a deliberate operation of the conditions by the researcher. In this process, a pre-determined set of conditions, called independent variable or treatment variable is imposed on the subjects of experiment. In the present study computer based modules for teaching of values was independent variable.

3.   **Observation.** In the experiment, the researcher observes the effect of the manipulation of the independent variable on the dependent variable. In the present study the effect of computer based modules was observed and tested by the

significant difference in average value score of Value Clarification Test.

4.   **Replication.** Replication is a matter of conduction a number of sub experiments, instead of one experiment only, within the framework of the same experimental design. The experiment was repeated in DSVK High School, Jasdan. Time table for main experiment and replication is given in table 5.1 and 5.2.

CHAPTER – 6
DATA ANALYSIS AND INTERPRETATION

6.1 INTRODUCTION

Data analysis and interpretation is an important stage in any research. After the data are collected, the researcher turns his focus of attention on their analysis. The analysis of data involves a number of closely related operations which are performed with the purpose of summarizing the collected data and organizing them in such a manner that they will yield answer to the questions or hypothesis in research.

Analysis means the categorizing, ordering, manipulating, and summarizing of data to obtain answers of research's question.

-   F.N.Kerlinger

Analysis and interpretation of the collected data is the most important step in the research processes. This process requires alert, flexible and open mind.

-   Hoper and Borg

In present study researcher had derived and classified values from the supplementary Reader book of English of standard XII, and also prepared computer based modules for teaching of values and tested its effectiveness. Therefore it is of both type i.e. first part is descriptive and second part is experimental.

In this chapter the analysis of the qualitative data and quantitative data which was obtained before experiment and after experiment is done.

Based on the objective of the study the derived values were analysing as describing.

6.2 REFERENCE SENTENCES FROM THESUPPLEMENTARY READER BOOK

In the present research the first objective was to identify the reference sentences from the supplementary Reader book of English of standard XII. Total forty one reference sentences were identified from ten Reads. The reference sentences of each Read were as describing.

6.2.1 Reference sentences from Read – 1.

From Read-1, six reference sentences were identified, which are as describing.

1. One day he noticed that sparrows he had shot at had a yellow throat. He couldn't hold (was unable to stop) his curiosity and approached his uncle.

2. He decided to study further to acquire eligibility (ability to do something /requirement) for the job. Salim went to Germany and got trained under Professor Stresemann, an acknowledged ornithologist in Berlin.

3. He went to the Bombay Natural History Society (BNHS) and offered his free services for conducting regional ornithological surveys.

4. It was his sincerity that won him many awards and medals from all over the world including the Padma Shree and Padma Vibhusana.

5. Let's pay a tribute to the Birdman by leaning to identify a few birds around us.

6. Salim Ali was a true nature lover and his love for the wildlife is expressed in his autobiography (*The Fall of a Sparrow*) where he calls the wildlife a capital, an asset and says,

6.2.2   Reference sentences from Read – 2.

From Read-2, six reference sentences were identified, which are as describing.

1. Mansi thought of the man and admired his patience for putting up with her constant parade of words.

2. Mansi gazed at (kept looking) them several times as she moved through the various rooms of art.

3. "He's a brave man". The clerk at the counter said." Most of us would give up if we were blinded at such a young age.

4. "His wife describes each painting through his mind's eye. So he can see."

5. She saw the patience of young wife describing paintings to a person without sight and the courage of a husband who would not allow blindness to alter his life.

6. Mansi witnessed the love shared by the two people as she watched this couple walk away with their arms interwined.

6.2.3   Reference sentences from Read – 3.

From Read-3, eight reference sentences were identified, which are as describing.

1. Often I returned home from soccer field after heavy practice to study until the early of the morning.

2. My team had been under vigorous (tough) physical training for the past four years in anticipation of this day.

3. I entered the game with the mind-set that the title was in our hands.

4. We deserved it because our desire to win was great!

5. I took a deep breath and reassured myself that I would give this game best of my abilities as if it were the last game I ever played.

6. The score was still tied at one to one until I received the ball with one minute to go. I needed to put the ball in the net, and I did just that, making the final score two to one. But it didn't go exactly as planned.

7. I found myself in a hospital bed, surrounded by family, friends and teammates.

8. Not only did we win, but I was able to discover a new level within. I guess I gained two victories that day.

6.2.4   Reference sentences from Read– 4.

From Read-4, five reference sentences were identified, which are as describing.

1. The combination of my self-criticism, low self-confidence and bad self-image was   staring to destroy the life I wanted to build for myself.

2. I had to conquer (overcome) my low self-esteem (love for the self). I had no other option.

3. One day I made a decision to change, and I started to Read everything I could about self-help.

4. My confidence grew and I began to see challenges as opportunities to move forward and succeed.

5. I have more friends and can rely on them when I feel myself slipping back to where I was before.

6.2.5   Reference sentences from Read– 5

From Read-5, one reference sentence was obtained, which is as describing.

1. My darling daughter,

   In her ecstasy,

   Is busy drawing

   Strange pictures.

6.2.6   Reference sentences from Read – 6

From Read-6, two reference sentences were identified, which are as describing.

1. I have loved family friends, nature, animals, music and many other things.

2. She continues to appreciate nature and the small bit of life.

6.2.7   Reference sentences from Read – 7

From Read-7, two reference sentences were identified, which are as describing.

1. There was once a king. If anyone committed a serious crime in the kingdom, the king did not condemn (give punishment) him to death.

2. The king had a very beautiful daughter. One day he found out that she had fallen in love with a poor young soldier in his army.

6.2.8   Reference sentences from Read – 8

From Read-8, six reference sentences were identified, which are as describing.

1. In bringing me and Asmi up, you had built self-esteem first and our house later. You had finger-paint (painting the fingers) more and pointed the finger less.

2. For last several years, I have been talking about my freedom.

3. I need you both to be with me and understand me about my decisions regarding what's wrong and what's right. I wish to try out my ways to deal with the situation around me.

4. Mummy…Pappa, I know, you have a right to suggest what fits her personality the best. But as 'understanding persons' let us respect her feelings and her wishes.

5. I hope you also want Asmi to venture on the path of life with her own maturity. Trust in her abilities and a little encouragement will facilitate her to learn how to respond to changing situations.

6. You both have contributed to my 'understanding'. I love you both for your wise, timely counsel (advise)

and friendly attitude. I am sure we will live as a happy family 'forever'.

6.2.9   Reference sentences from Read – 9

From Read-9, two reference sentences were identified, which are as describing.

1. "You are hardworking and scoring very well in all the subjects then way are you so much worried over something? If you have any problem you can share it with me."

2. "Thanks to the internet. It's not at all a problem now. Come with me. Within half an hour, you will be free from your worries. By the way, do you have an access to the internet?"

6.2.10   Reference sentences from Read – 10

From Read-10, three reference sentences were identified, which are as describing.

1. You say the sun shines bright;

   I feel him warm, but how can he

   Or make it day or night?

2. With heavy sighs I often hear

   You mourn your hapless woe;

   But sure with patience I can bear

   A loss I ne'er can know.

3. Then let not what I cannot have

    My cheer of mind destroys:

    Whilst thus I sing, I am a king,

    Although a poor blind boy.

6.3   VALUES EMERGING FROM THE SUPPLEMENTARY READER BOOK AND ITS TYPE

In the present research the second and third objectives were to identify the value emerging from the supplementary Reader book of English of standard XII and its type. There were twenty eight values identified from ten Reads which are classified into six types. Values emerging and its type are presented as describing.

6.3.1 Values emerging from Read-1 and its type. From Read-1 there were six values identified from six reference sentences. The values and its type were tabulated in table-6.1.

Table - 6.1

Values emerging from Read – 1 and its type.

Read Name	Values Emerging	Type of Value
The Birdman of India	Curiosity	Personal Value
	Quest for Knowledge	Spiritual Value
	Helpfulness	Personal Value
	Dignity of the Individual	Social Value
	Kindness to Animal	Social Value
	Gratitude	Personal Value

While studying table 6.1, six values were identified from Read -1. The types of values were: Social Value – 2. Spiritual Value – 1, Personal Value – 3.

6.3.2 Values emerging from Read-2 and its type. From Read -2 there were three values identified from two reference sentences. The values and its type were tabulated in table-6.2.

Table - 6.2

Values emerging from Read– 2 and its type.

Read Name	Values Emerging	Type of Value
Her Words, His Vision	Patience	Moral Value
	Curiosity	Personal Value
	Courage	Personal Value
	Consideration for others	Personal Value
	Self-respect	Personal Value
	Compassion	Social Value

While studying table 6.2, six values were identified from Read - 2. The types of values were: Moral Value – 1, Personal Value – 4, and Social Value – 1.

6.3.3 Values emerging from Read - 3 and its type.

From Read-3 there were eight values identified from four reference sentences. The values and its type were tabulated in table-6.3.

Table - 6.3

Values emerging from Read– 3 and its type.

Read Name	Values Emerging	Type of Value
Final Game	Self-Study	Personal Value
	Dignity of Manual Work	Social Value
	Self-confidence	Personal Value

	Team-work	Moral Value
	Self-help	Personal Value
	Curiosity	Personal Value
	Friendship	Social Value
	Self-control	Personal Value

While studying table 6.3, eight values were identified from Read - 3. The types of values were: Personal Value – 5, Social Value – 2, and Moral Value – 1.

6.3.4 Values emerging from Read-4 and its type. From Read-4 there were five values identified from four reference sentences. The values and its type were tabulated in table-6.4.

Table - 6.4

Values emerging from Read– 4 and its type.

Read Name	Values Emerging	Type of Value
	Initiative	Personal Value
	Self-respect	Personal Value
I Love Me	Self-help	Personal Value
	Self-confidence	Personal Value
	Friendship	Social Value

While studying table 6.4, five values were identified from Read - 4. The types of values were: Personal Value – 4, and Social Value – 1.

6.3.5 Values emerging from Read-5 and its type. From Read-5 there was one value identified from one reference sentence. The value and it type was tabulated in table-6.5.

Table - 6.5

Values emerging from Read– 5 and it type.

Read Name	Values Emerging	Type of Value
Pencil	Ecstasy	Spiritual Value

While studying table 6.5, one value was identified from Read - 5. The type of value was: Spiritual Value – 1.

6.3.6 Values emerging from Read-6 and its type. From Read-6 there were three values identified from three reference sentences. The values and its type were tabulated in table-6.6.

Table - 6.6

Values emerging from Read– 6 and its type.

Read Name	Values Emerging	Type of Value
6. I Miss You, Mother	Universal Love	Global Value
	Kindness to Animals	Social Value

While studying table 6.6, two values were identified from Read- 6. The types of values were: Global Value – 1 and Social Value – 1.

6.3.7 Values emerging from Read-7 and its type. From Read-7 there were two values identified from two reference sentences. The values and its type were tabulated in table-6.7.

Table - 6.7

Values emerging from Read– 7 and its type.

Read Name	Values Emerging	Type of Value
7. The Princess and The Tiger	Justice	Social Value
	Love	Personal Value

While studying table 6.7, two values were identified from Read- 7. The types of values were: Social Value – 1 and Personal Value - 1.

6.3.8 Values emerging from Read-8 and its type. From Read-8 there were six values identified from six reference sentences. The values and its type were tabulated in table-6.8.

Table - 6.8

Values emerging from Read– 7 and its type.

Read Name	Values Emerging	Type of Value
8. Ananya Writes to His Parents	Self-respect	Personal Value
	Freedom	Political Value
	Common Good	Social Value
	Consideration for others	Personal Value
	Faithfulness	Personal Value
	Respect for Others	Moral Value

While studying table 6.8, six values were identified from Read-8. The types of values were: Moral Value – 1, Personal Value -3, Political Value-1 and Social Value - 1.

6.3.9 Values emerging from Read-9 and its type. From Read-9 there were two values identified from two reference sentences. The values and its type were tabulated in table-6.9.

Table - 6.9

Values emerging from Read– 9 and its type.

Read Name	Values Emerging	Type of Value
9. Vismay @ Search	Co-Operation	Social Value
	Quest for Knowledge	Spiritual Value

While studying table 6.9, two values were identified from Read- 9. The types of values were: Social Value – 1 and Spiritual Value - 1.

Table - 6.10

Values emerging from Read– 10 and its type.

Read Name	Values Emerging	Type of Value
10. The Blind Boy	Self-Reliance	Personal Value
	Patience	Personal Value
	Faithfulness	Personal Value

While studying table 6.10, three values were identified from Read- 10. The types of values were: Personal Value – 3.

6.4 CLASSIFICATION OF VALUES EMERGING FROM SUPPLEMENTARY READER BOOK 'LAPWING'

In the present research the fourth aim was to classify the values emerging from supplementary Reader book 'Lapwing' of English of standard XII. From ten Reads total forty one values were classified. These values were classified based on the classification given by 1996 National Education Policy. The Values classification was tabulated in table 6.11.

Table - 6.11

Classification of Values

While studying table 6.11, total forty one values were classified from ten Reads of which were classified into six types. Number of values in each type is: Spiritual Values – 3, Moral Values – 3, Social Values – 10, Global Values – 1, Personal Values – 23 and Political Values – 1.

6.5   MEANING OF VALUES EMERGING FROM SUPPLEMENTARY READER BOOK.

In the present study the fifth objective was to give meaning of values emerging from supplementary Reader book of English of standard XII. There were total twenty eight values identified from ten Reads, whose meaning are as describing.

11. Consideration for Others

Consideration is a kind way of behaving that shows you care about other people's feelings and needs. It is careful thought before making a decision or judgement about something.

12. Co-operation

Co-operation is a situation in which people or organizations work together to achieve a <u>result</u> that will <u>benefit</u> all of them. It is an act or instance of working or acting together for a common purpose or benefit.

13. Compassion

Compassion is a feeling of deep sympathy and sorrow for another who is stricken by misfortune, accompanied by a strong desire to alleviate the suffering.

14. Common Good

Common good is the work done to benefit or interest of all people in society or in a group. Common goods always benefits human race or society as a whole.

15.Courage

Courage is the quality of mind or spirit that enables a person to face difficulty, danger, pain etc. without fear. It is ability to something that frightens one.

16.Curiosity

Curiosity is a quality related to inquisitive thinking such as exploration, investigation, and learning, evident by observation in human and animal species. Curiosity is heavily associated with all aspects of human development, in which derives the process of learning and desire to acquire knowledge and skill.

17.Dignity of manual work

Dignity of Manual Work is a work in which you use your hands or your physical strength rather than your mind in which a way of appearing or behaving that suggest seriousness and self-control. It is a quality of being worthy of honour.

18.Ecstasy

Ecstasy is a state of extreme happiness, especially when feeling pleasure. It suggests an intensification of emotion so powerful as to produce a trancelike dissociation from all but the single overpowering feeling.

19. Friendship

Friendship is a relation where two individual or a group of people, share, cares and respect each other. They also guide if one is going in wrong direction and also helps in tough time without any expectation.

20. Faithfulness

Faithfulness is the quality of being faithful. It is showing true & constant support or loyalty towards duty or a person.

21. Freedom

Freedom is the state of being free or at liberty rather than in confinement or under physical restraint. It stands for something greater than just the right to act however I choose. It also stands for securing to everyone an equal opportunity for life, liberty, and the pursuit of happiness.

22. Gratitude

Gratitude is a feeling of appreciation or thanks towards others. It is a feeling or attitude in acknowledgment of a benefit that one has received or will receive.

23. Helpfulness

Helpfulness is the quality of being <u>helpful</u>. It means trying to make life a little easier for other people. If we are paying attention, we notice when someone else is struggling –to open a door, to complete a task, or even to go through the dying process with grace and dignity. We move instinctively to ease the struggle – lending ourselves whether for a moment or a lifetime to serve their purpose.

24. Initiative

Initiative is a personal quality or power to begin or to follow through, energetically with a plan or task with determination. In simpler words initiative is the ability to act or take charge before others do.

25. Justice

Justice is a concept of moral rightness based on ethics, rationality, law equality and fairness. It is also quality of being fair.

26. Kindness to Animal

Kindness to animals is the felling to protect the animals. It includes prohibition of hunting or killing of animals for human pleasure, ornaments, clothes etc.

27. Love

Love is a strong affection for another arising out of kinship or personal ties. It is an affection and tenderness felt by <u>lovers. It is an</u> affection based on admiration, benevolence, or common interests.

28. Patience

Patience is an ability or willingness to suppress restlessness or annoyance when confronted with delay. It is the quality of being patient, as the bearing of provocation, annoyance, misfortune, or pain without complaint, loss of temper, irritation.

29. Quest for knowledge

Quest for knowledge is the act or an instance of looking for or seeking or search for knowledge. It is a search or pursuit made in order to find or obtain knowledge.

30. Respect for others

Respect is a feeling of admiring someone or something that is good, valuable, importance, etc. It is feeling or understanding that someone or something is important, serious, etc. It is a particular way of thinking about or looking at something.

31.   Self Help

Self-help is the use of one's own efforts and resources to achieve things without relying on others. It is reduction in the role of the state and an increasing reliance on self-help. *It is the action or process of bettering oneself or overcoming one's problems without the aid of others.*

32. Self-respect

Self-respect is a proper respect for oneself as a human being. It is regarding for one's own standing or position.

33. Self-confidence

Self-confidence is a feeling of trust in one's abilities, qualities, and judgement. It is a feeling of trust in self. To be self-confident is to have confidence in yourself. Self-confident people don't doubt themselves.

34. Self-control

Self-control is the quality that allows you to stop yourself from doing things you want to do but that might not be in your best interest.

35. Self-reliance

Self- reliance is the ability to depend on yourself to get things done and to meet your own needs. It is on one's own judgment, abilities, etc. The <u>capacity</u> is to <u>rely</u> on one's own <u>capabilities</u> and to <u>manage</u> one's own <u>affairs independently.</u>

36. Self- study

37. Self-study is the study of something by oneself, as through books, records, etc. without direct supervision or attendance in a class. It is the study of something by oneself and self-examination.

38. Teamwork

Teamwork is the process of working collaboratively with a group of people in order to achieve a goal. It is a combined action of a group of people especially when effective and efficient.

39. Universal love

Universal love is a love without expectations; impersonal love; doing good works. These are spiritual words, spiritual values. It gives us true understanding and helps us live it truly. Love to all.

6.6 LEARNING OUTCOME OF VALUES EMERGING FROM SUPPLEMENTARY READER BOOK.

In the present research the sixth objective was to explain learning outcome of values emerging from supplementary Reader book of English of standard XII. Total twenty eight values were identified from ten Reads. Learning outcome for each value is tabulated in table 6.12.

6.7 EFFECTIVENESS OF COMPUTER BASED MODULES FOR TEACHING OF VALUES EMERGING FROM SUPPLEMENTARY READER BOOK.

In the present research seventh and eighth objective was to prepare and test the Effectiveness of computer based modules for teaching of values emerging from supplementary Reader book 'Lapwing' of English subject of Standard XII. After derivation and classification of values computer based modules for teaching of values were prepared for first four Reads, and its effectiveness was tested. The experiment was conducted in standard - XII of Shri M.B. Ajmera High School of all pre-test was given to the students and then they were shown computer based modules for teaching of values. After module got over post-test was given. To test effectiveness value score of pre-test of Value Clarification Test and value score of post-test of Value Clarification Test were taken and t-test was used for analysis. The outcome is shown in table 6.13.

Table 6.13

t – Value of Main Experiment

Test	Number of Students	Average	Standard Deviation	t-value
Pre-Test	35	3.43	2.61	53.79
Post-	35			

Test		44.77	4.92	

Significant at 0.01 levels

Table 6.13 indicates that average value score of post-test was 44.77 and standard deviation was 4.92. While average value score of pre-test was 3.43 and standard deviation was 2.61 and t-value was 53.79 which was significant at 0.01 level. Thus the hypothesis of study was not accepted. That is computer based modules were effective for teaching of values.

6.8   REPLICATION

The term 'replication' is really a fusion of two words, namely duplication and repetition. It refers to the deliberate repetition of an experiment, using a nearly identical procedure with different set of subjects, in a different setting at different time.

Winer has similarly said, "A replication of an experiment is an independent repetition under as nearly identical conditions as the nature of the experimental material will permit". Replication permits a person in revalidating a previous study.

The experiment was replicated in DSVK High School. The experiment was conducted in standard - XII of DSVK High School. First of all pre-test was given to the students and then they were shown computer based modules for teaching of values. After module got over post-test was given. To test effectiveness value score of pre-test and value score of post-test were taken and t-test was used for analysis. The outcome is shown in table 6.14.

Table 6.14

t – Value of Replicated Experiment

Test	Number of Students	Average	Standard Deviation	t-value
Pre-Test	35	4.51	2.06	39.55
Post-Test	35	43.91	6.56	

Significant at 0.01 levels

Table 6.14 indicates that average value score of post-test was 43.91 and standard deviation was 6.56. While average value score of pre-test was 4.51 and standard deviation was 2.06 and t-value was 39.55 which was significant at 0.01 level. Thus the hypothesis of study was not accepted. That is computer based modules were effective for teaching of values.

CHAPTER – 7

FINDINGS, IMPLICATIONS AND RECOMMENDATIONS

7.1 INTRODUCTION

The researcher has made an attempt to justify the chapter by giving necessary details of the summary of the study, test on null hypothesis, conclusion of the study, implications and future recommendations.

7.2 SUMMARY OF THE STUDY

In present study researcher had prepared computer based modules for teaching value and tested its effectiveness using experimental method.

Following steps were followed:

1. First Ten Reads of the supplementary reader book `Lapwing' of English of standard XII were   selected for the study. The researcher had read all the Reads in reference with values identification.

2. Researcher had separated out those sentences from which values were emerging. There were total forty one reference sentences from ten Reads.

3. After identification of reference sentences researcher had identified value or values emerging from reference

sentences. Twenty eight values were identified from forty one reference sentences.

4. After identification of value, researcher had found out its type, twenty eight values were classified into six different types of values.

5. Read wise classification of values was done based on the value type. After classification meaning and learning outcome of each value was found out, with the help of expert opinion. There were total fifty five learning outcome found out for twenty eight values.

6. Computer based modules were prepared for teaching of values for first four Reads. For this, software like movie maker, power point, and Ms-word were used.

7. To test the effectiveness of the computer based module by experimental method, a sample of thirty five students of standard XII of Shree M.B. Ajmera High School, were taken who were given a value clarification test as a pre-test. After pre-test computer based modules were shown to them and at the end of each read a value clarification test as a post test was also taken.

8. The experiment was repeated on the sample of thirty five students of standard XII of DSVK High School.

10. Value Score was obtained for both the pre-test and post-test. T-test was used as statistical technique to compare value score of pre-test and post- test. After obtaining t-value null hypothesis was interpreted.

7.3 INTERPRETATION FOR HYPOTHESIS

Null hypothesis of present study was, '**There will be no significant difference between average value score obtained by students of Std. XII of pre-test and post-test as Value Clarification Test.**'

To test this hypothesis t-value was found to be 53.79 in main experiment and 39.55 in replication, which was significant at 0.01 level, so null hypothesis was rejected. Hence the computer based modules for teaching values was found effective.

7.4 CONCLUSION OF THE STUDY

Conclusions of the study on the interpretations obtained at the end of testing of hypothesis are as follow.

Computer based modules were prepared to teach and inculcate the values. At the end of experiment it is found that computer based modules for teaching values is effective.

Also the same findings were obtained in replication of the experiment.

Computer based modules can enhance grasping and understanding of the students and help them in retention through graphics, animated stories, photos, picture story, videos etc. This will help in developing better understanding about values.

Also students like to learn through computer based teaching learning process as it becomes easy to fix the content by this method.

7.5 FINDINGS OF THE RESEARCH

This research was conducted to examine the effectiveness of computer based modules for teaching of values in English of standard XII at higher secondary level. For this the supplementary reader book 'Lapwing' of English is selected and values were derived for first ten Reads. Then computer based modules were prepared using the software of movie maker for four reads. In the experiment value clarification test as a pre-test is conducted and then computer based modules were shown and then value clarification test as a post test was conducted. Analysis was done by t-test and computer based modules found to be effective.

By using this type of computer based modules teachers can bring newness in teacher learning process and enhance the retention of the students.

7.6 RESEARCH IMPLICATIONS

On the basis of the findings of the research, the researcher would like to present certain implications for the study.

1. Languages like English can be a good source to develop an understanding for values in the students.

2. Computer based modules are effective in value teaching also, as it helps in building up better understanding of values in students.

3. The result of present study will be useful for teacher to develop the value in the future generation students.

4.   By computer based modules newness in teaching learning process can be brought about and this will make the students more positive towards subjects.

5.   The education board can make the value manual which can serve as ready tool for value teaching.

7.6 RECOMMENDATIONS FOR THE FUTURE RESEARCHES

On the basis of the review of earlier researches, the result obtained at the end of this research and the experiment during the research the researcher wants to give recommendations for the future researches, which are as follow.

1.   Other subjects like Hindi, Gujarati and Social Sciences are also good source of values; hence research can be conducted by taking the above subjects.

2.   The approach of a teacher towards the subject who teaches through computer based modules and the approach of a teacher towards the subject who teaches through traditional teaching method can be compared.

3.   During teaching through computer based modules the type of relationship between slow learner students and bright students should be examined.

4.   Other software like flash can also be used to prepare computer based modules.

5.   Present work can be repeated using other population and geographical areas.

6. Effectiveness of computer based modules can be compared with project

method,   Role play method or any other method in teaching values.

Thus, in the present chapter the researcher discussed about the summary of the research work, findings, implications and recommendations were made for the future research.

REFERENCES

Ambasana, A.D. (2006). **A Visual Guide to SPSS for Windows.** Rajkot : Department of Education, Saurashtra University.

Ambasana, A.D. (2002). **Know Your Computer.** (Guj) Department of Education: Saurashtra University

Borg W.R. & Gall, M.D. (1999). **Educational Research.** New Delhi : Prentice Hall of India Pvt. Ltd.

Buch, M.B. (Ed.) (1974). **A Survey of Research in Education.** Baroda: Centre of   Advance Study in Education.

.... (Ed.) (1979). **Second Survey of Research in Education.** Baroda: Centre   of   Advance   Study   in Education.

.... (Ed.) (1987). **Third Survey of Research in Education.** Baroda: Centre of   Advance Study in Education.

.... (Ed.) (1991). **Fourth Survey of Research In Education.** Baroda: Centre   of   Advance   Study   in Education.

Desai, H.G (1979). **Style Manual for Dissertation/Theses.** Rajkot : Saurashtra   University.

Director, Gujarat State Education Board (2010). `Lapwing' **supplementary reader book of English subject of Standard – XII.** Gandhinagar; Gujarat State Education Board.

Frankel, J.B. (1977). **How to Teach About Values.** New Delhi : Prentice Hall of   India Pvt. Ltd.Gawande,

E.N. (2008). **Value Oriented Education: Vision for Better Living.** New   Delhi: Sarup & Sons.

Goel, B.R. (1983). **Documents on Social, Moral and Spiritual Values.** New Delhi: N.C.E.R.T.

Joshi, H.O (1998). **Value Education.** (Guj). Rajkot: Manorama Prakashan.

.... (1998). **Educational Philosophy.** (Guj). Rajkot: Vasuki Printing Press.

.... (2004). **Education of Values.** (Guj). Rajkot: Manorama Prakashan.

Kellerman, D.P. (1988). **New Webster's Dictionary of the English Language.** New Delhi: Surjit Publications.

Kothari, C. R. (2014). **Research Methodology.** New Delhi: New Age International (P) Limited .

Lara, R.M. (1976). **Values in a Developing Country with Special Reference to India.** Ambala Cantt: Indian PublicationPathak, R.C. (1972). **Bhargava's English Dictionary.** New Delhi: Bhargav Publications.

Promila, K. (2008). **"Value Education: based on all religions of the world".** Kalpaz Publishers, Delhi.

Ramanuj, B.B.(2004). **Value Education Through Teaching Various Subjects at Secondary Level.** (Guj). Rajkot: Pravin Pustak Bhandar.

Ruhela, S.P. (1986). **Human Values and Education.** New Delhi: Sterling Publisher.

Shukla, S. (2000). **Excel and Data Analysis (Guj.).** Ahmedabad: Kshiti Publication .

Simon, S., Howe, L., & Kirschenbaum, H. (1972). **Values clarification: A handbook of practical strategies for teachers and students.** New York: Hart.

Uchat, D.A. (1998). **How to Write Research Report.** (Guj). Rajkot: Nijinn Psycho Centre.

....................(2000). **Four Special Methods of Research.** (Guj). Rajkot: Saurashtra University.

....................(2006). **Qualitative Research.** (Guj). Rajkot: Saurashtra University.

....................(2009). **Research Methodology in Education and Social Sciences.** (Guj). Ahmedabad: Sahitya Mudralaya.

Venkataiah, N. (2008). **Research in Value Education**. New Delhi; A.P.H. Publishing House.

Yuktananda, S. (1989). **Values ourselves; Value systems and human relationship.**

Vivekananda Nidhi, Calcutta.

THESIS

Andhariya, H. (2008). **The Effectiveness of Computer Based Program for the Unit of Factorization.** Bhavnagar University, Education Department. Bhavnagar: Unpublished.

Dave, J. (2009). **The Effectiveness of Value Identification Model in Teaching of Social Science of Standard IX.** Saurashtra University, Education Department. Rajkot: Unpublished.

Gohel, M. (2002). **A study of Values Covered in Upnishadas.** Saurashtra University, Education Department. Rajkot: Unpublished.

Rose, S. (2005). **The Effectiveness of Computer Assised Teaching Software in Low Achievement students.** M.S. University, Education Department. Vadodara: Unpublished.

DISSERTATION

Chavda, R. (1995). **Quality Emerging from Children Stories of Gijubhai Badheka.** Saurashtra University, Education Department. Rajkot: Unpublished M.Ed. dissertation.

Dalwadi. N. (2001). **Development of Computer Assisted Instruction in Science for the Students of Standard IX.** M. S. University, Baroda: Unpublished M.Ed. dissertation.

Joshi, C. L. (1992). **The Construction and Try-out of Networks for some Topics of Physics for Standard XII Science Stream.** South Gujarat University Surat: Unpublished M.Ed. Dissertation.

Huitt, W. (2004). **Values. Educational Psychology Interactive**. Valdosta, GA: Valdosta State University. Retrieved 2/7/2010, from http://www.edpsycinteractive.org

Kumar, Pradeep (2009). **Role of value education in contemporary society**.   Retrieved on September 29, 2010 from   http://www.indiastudychannel.com/forum/24476 Role-Value-Education-Contemporary-Society.aspx

Kumta, J. (2012). **Value Education: what can be done?** www.teachersofndia.org

Pelgrum, W. J., Law, N. (2003). **"ICT in Education around the World: Trends, Problems and Prospects"** UNESCO-International   Institute   for   Educational Planning.Available:www.worldcatlibraries.org

Saverinus Kaka, S.Pd. (2008). **"The Role of ICT in Education Sector"** Victoria L. Tinio., ICT   in Education. July 25, 2008.

Sanyal, B. C. **Need for Value based Education in twenty first Century.** www.herenow4u.de (retrieved on 12 August, 2014)

Seetharam, A. R. (2014) **Concept and Objective of Value Education.** www.ncte-india.org (retrieved on 14 August, 2014)

Sindhvani, A. (2013). **Value in Higher Education: Need and Importance.** www.confabjournals.com

Vaishu, (2013). **Importance of Value based Education**. www.studymode.com

Vernal, L. and Paily M.U. (2004). **ICT in Teacher Education : A case study.** University News. 42(39). 1-7

UNESCO   (2002).   **Information and Communication Technologies in Teacher Education. A Planning Guide**: UNESCO Publication.

UNESCO (2008). **ICT Competency Standards for Teachers.** UNESCO.

WEB SITE
www.clip.dj
www.edpsycinteractive.org
www.google.com
www.googlebooks.com
www.ncert.nic.in
www.teachersofndia.org
www.youtube.com
www.wikipedia.com
www.worldcatlibraries.org
www.inflibnet.ac.in